Praise for
The Emerging Cooperative Economy

"Your book is amazing! It is a sweeping look at how we arrived at today, and it presents a blueprint for survival – not just survival, but a world with hope, rooted in a cooperative economy."

Mark Lefebvre, Former President and CEO of Stanton & Lee Publishers

"I always find your capacity for synthesis admirable, allowing you to reconstruct long phases of our history in just a few pages. This can certainly be of help to those who seek an introduction that will orient them with regard to the major trends and problems of our world."

Gianluca Salvatori, Secretary General of the European Research Institute on Cooperative and Social Enterprises (EURICSE) and Secretary General of the Social Italy Foundation

"E.G. Nadeau touches on the key issues we need to consider for an improved economy in which co-operatives and other forms of economic democracy contribute to a more hopeful world. E.G. envisions a world where ownership of the economy is distributed more fairly, and economic output shared far more widely.

"As I look at our world, it seems clear that we must have the courage to rethink how our national and global economies function. With economic inequality and environmental disruption growing around the world, the ability of our economy to provide people with the basics of life is declining. Climate change is also a product of the economy. E.G. Nadeau's call for growing alternatives to our current economic order is a valuable contribution to an urgent call to action."

Tom Webb, Cofounder of The International Centre for Co-operative Management, St. Mary's University

"In his latest book, *The Emerging Cooperative Economy,* E.G. Nadeau has thoroughly researched and compiled UN benchmarks, reports from worldwide agencies, and stories about individuals, grassroots programs, and business models around the world that are making a positive impact."

Jill Stevenson, Cooperative Communicator

The Emerging Cooperative Economy:

Improving Democracy, Quality of Life, and the Environment by 2050

Published by E.G. Nadeau, Ph.D.
egnadeau3@gmail.com
thecooperativesociety.org
Madison, Wisconsin

The Emerging Cooperative Economy
E.G. Nadeau, Ph.D.
1. Cooperation
2. Cooperatives
3. Cooperative economy
4. Political democracy
5. Economic democracy
6. Quality of life
7. Environmental sustainability

Other books by E.G. Nadeau:
- *Cooperation Works! How People Are Using Cooperative Action to Rebuild Communities and Revitalize the Economy*, (with David J. Thompson), 1997
- *The Cooperative Solution: How the United States can tame recessions, reduce inequality, and protect the environment*, 2012
- *The Cooperative Society: The Next Stage of Human History* (with Luc Nadeau), first edition, 2016; second edition, 2018
- *Strengthening the Cooperative Community*, 2021

ISBN 979-8-9907177-0-1
Printed in the United States of America
Cover artwork by Luc Nadeau
First printing June 2024

To my grandchildren –
Maia, Alex, Remy, and Hollis
and
To all of our descendants who will live with the consequences
of what we do (and don't do) in the next quarter century

Preface

During my college days studying sociology in the 1960s, I learned that people can be the subjects of history as well as its objects. We can intentionally shape the society in which we live, and the economy that determines the distribution of wealth and other resources. What we often take as "givens" are not, in fact, pre-ordained rules and relationships.[1]

In many ways, human history is the story of people struggling to improve the quality of life for themselves, their children and, sometimes, their communities. Our species began about 300,000 years ago as two-legged mammals trying to stay alive and pro-create in a physical world fraught with danger. Now, our greatest danger is ourselves. As cartoonist Walt Kelly put it, "We have met the enemy and he is us."[2] To put that quote in a more positive light, our fate is in our own hands. What we do in the next several decades to strengthen democracy, reduce social and economic inequality, and address the problems of human-made climate change will affect our descendants and the state of the planet for the next century or more.

In 2012, I wrote a book entitled *The Cooperative Solution: How the United States can tame recessions, reduce inequality, and protect the environment.*[3] The United Nations had designated 2012 as "The International Year of Cooperatives," and I wanted to make a contribution to the discussion taking place that year about this democratically owned and controlled business model. The book made the case that economic democracy (exemplified by cooperatives) was an essential, but undervalued, complement to political democracy in the United States.

I realized while researching and writing *The Cooperative Solution* that I was only telling part of the story and that someday I wanted to tell more of it. The broader story? What a transition to a more cooperative economy in the 21st century might look like, not only in the United States, but as a worldwide paradigm shift. Telling that story is the purpose of this book.

The basic theme of *The Cooperative Economy* (my shorthand name for this book) is that the world today is characterized by concentrated economic and political power, extreme inequality in access to basic goods and services, and environmental devastation. However, we are not stuck with such a set of dysfunctional economies forever. During the coming decades, we can transition to an international economic landscape based on increasing political and economic democracy, meeting human needs, and sustaining the environment.

In October 2023, the UN General Assembly designated 2025 as a second International Year of Cooperatives in the 21st century.[4] More about the 2025 Year of Cooperatives in chapter 8.

This book presents a possible path for moving toward a more cooperative society and economy by 2050.

—*E.G. Nadeau, Ph.D.*

Acknowledgments

I would especially like to thank The Cooperative Society Project team for all their help in preparing this book for publication:

- Sue Filbin: primary editing, design, and layout
- Isaac Nadeau: editing, advice on content and design
- Luc Nadeau: editing, cover artwork, and advice on content and design
- Jill Stevenson: social media and communications
- Alan Wilfahrt: production and technology direction

Many other people provided valuable comments on, and contributed to the editing of, this book. I am grateful to all of them. Key advisers, colleagues, and friends include: Michael Cunningham, Steve Dubb, Louis Fortis, Dave Grace, Mark Lefebvre, Gianluca Salvatori, Charles Sanders, Michael Sherraden, Kate Sumberg, Walden Swanson, Todd Thompson, Tom Webb, and Tony Webster.

In the end, I take full responsibility for the information, analyses, recommendations, and conclusions presented in the book, and for any errors that may have crept in along the way.

Table of Contents

The Emerging Cooperative Economy: Improving Democracy, Quality of Life, and the Environment by 2050

Conclusion

Introduction

I have been researching, promoting, writing, and teaching about cooperatives and cooperation for more than 50 years.

This book is about our economic past and present, and our potential to transition to a more cooperative world economy in the 21st century. The intended readership is quite broad, ranging from secondary school students to policymakers, academics, and others interested in the trajectory of human economies from the beginning of our species to possible options in the decades ahead.

What do I mean by a cooperative economy? The short answer is: An economy that puts the well-being of the many ahead of the wealth and power of a few. This book provides a longer answer along with steps we can take to make the transition from an inequitable and unsustainable world economy to one based on meeting human needs and protecting the planet.

Recent scientific evidence indicates that homo sapiens or "modern humans"[5] emerged as a species in Africa about 300,000 years ago.[6] Since then, we have evolved to become the most dominant and invasive species on the planet.

How did we get from a few small, transient communities in Africa to more than eight billion people spread across the entire habitable world? Why is this human-dominated world so deeply flawed by the powerlessness and uncertainty that most of us feel, by the dramatic differences in the quality of our lives, and by the damage that we inflict on our physical environment? And what can we do to overcome these problems and transition to a more cooperative society and economy?

The purpose of this book is to suggest answers to these questions from an economic perspective. The word economy is derived from the Greek words "ecos" and "nemos" which together mean "management of the household."[7] Over time, the meaning of economy has evolved from meeting the needs of the household to those of the broader society and environment. I like both the origin and the historical evolution of the word economy. After all, the world is our home, and it is critically important that we learn how to better manage and sustain it.

Groups of humans have had millions of different economies over the millennia, and thousands today at local community, regional, national, and international levels. When I refer to the world economy in the book, it is essentially a summing up of all these economies and represents the dominant paradigm that characterizes them.

I have chosen to use the levels of political and economic democracy, quality of life, and environmental sustainability as a combined measure of a cooperative world economic paradigm. The primary purposes of this paradigm are: 1) to provide information on the evolution of human economies among local groups, and larger aggregations of us, all the way up to the world level; and 2) to make recommendations for transitioning to a predominance of cooperative economies in the world – with high levels of political and economic democracy, an adequate quality of life for all of us, and a sustainable relationship with the ecosystems that are, in fact, the households we inhabit.

The methodology of the book is to use both qualitative and quantitative information to describe the evolution of our diverse economies to date, and to propose a future set of more cooperative economies around the world. Much of the qualitative information is presented in the form of examples and stories.

Definitions

To explore the above themes, we need to have clear definitions of the key words and phrases used in the book. Following is a set of these definitions.

Political democracy

According to Wikipedia, "Democracy.... is a system of government in which state power is vested in the people or the general population of a state. ... In a direct democracy, the people have the direct authority to deliberate and decide legislation. In a representative democracy, the people choose governing officials through elections to do so. Who is considered part of 'the people' and how authority is shared among or delegated by the people has changed over time and at different rates in different countries."[8]

A more detailed definition and analysis of political democracy is presented in chapter 7.

Economic democracy

As quoted from Wikipedia: "Economic democracy.... is a socio-economic philosophy that proposes to shift ownership and decision-making power from corporate shareholders and corporate managers (such as a board of directors) to a larger group of public stakeholders that includes workers, consumers, suppliers, communities and the broader public. No single definition or approach encompasses economic democracy, but most proponents claim that modern property relations externalize costs, subordinate the general well-being to private profit and deny the polity a democratic voice in economic policy decisions."[9]

Steve Dubb, Ted Howard, and Sarah McKinley provide more nuanced definitions and analyses in their essay on "Economic Democracy."[10] The term is further defined and analyzed in chapter 8.

Cooperative enterprises

Cooperative enterprises are often referred to as the most prominent examples of economic democracy. The International Cooperative Alliance defines a *cooperative* as "an autonomous association of persons united voluntarily to meet their common economic, social and cultural needs and aspirations through a jointly owned and democratically controlled enterprise."[11] Note that part of the definition of a cooperative is that it is an "enterprise," in other words, a formally organized business.

Quality of life

Quality of life is defined by the Organization for Economic Cooperation and Development "as the well-being of [a] population in its various dimensions." The OECD goes on to provide a list of some of these dimensions: income and jobs, housing conditions, health, education, environmental quality, personal security, civic engagement and work-life balance.[12]

Note that civic engagement, as defined by Wikipedia, "...includes communities working together or individuals working alone in both political and non-political actions to protect public values or make a change in a community. The goal of civic engagement is to address public concerns and promote the quality of the community."[13] The concept of civic engagement is given special attention in the definition and analysis of quality of life as presented in chapter 9.

Environmental sustainability

Environmental sustainability is defined by the United Nations as "meeting the needs of the present without compromising the ability of future generations to meet their own needs."[14] As discussed in chapter 10, human ecology, "the study of the relationship between humans and their natural, social, and built environments,"[15] is an integral part of the definition and analysis of environmental sustainability.

Cooperation

As defined in the book, cooperation means "working together towards a shared aim."[16] In contrast to the above definition of a *cooperative enterprise*, the core definition of cooperation is a much broader social and economic concept. (This book focuses both on cooperatives as major components of a cooperative economy, and on cooperation as the primary way that individuals and groups interact in such an economy.)

Economy

An economy is "[a] system of production, distribution and consumption [of goods and services]."[17]

Market economy

A market economy is "an economic system in which economic decisions and the pricing of goods and services are guided by the interactions of. ... individual citizens and businesses. There may be some government intervention or central planning, but usually this term refers to an economy that is more market oriented in general."[18]

Mixed economy

A mixed economy is "an economy with a mixture of state and private enterprises. Some economic activities are carried out by individuals or firms taking independent economic decisions, coordinated by markets; others are carried on by organizations under state ownership and control, with some degree of centralized decision-taking. Most actual economies are mixed, in the sense of having substantial elements of both forms of economic organization."[19]

Cooperative economy

A cooperative economy is a system of production, distribution and consumption of goods and services that is primarily based on working together to achieve shared aims.[20]

Other definitions

I deliberately excluded capitalism, social democracy, socialism, and communism from the above list of definitions. These words are discussed and analyzed in chapter 5.

Organization of the book

The first section of the book is "Part I: Our Economic Past," which contains chapters on our chimpanzee relatives, human hunters and gatherers, the early stages of agriculture, and the rise and fall of empires leading to an increasingly integrated, but dysfunctional, world economy.

The second section of the book is "Part II: Toward a Cooperative World Economy," with chapters on our current world of mixed economies, the seeds of change present in these economies, and four chapters on increasing political democracy and economic democracy, reducing inequality, and creating a more sustainable environment. The final two chapters present four scenarios for the world economy in 2050, and a strategy for transitioning to a more cooperative world economy by mid-century.

One can view the book as two sets of essays. One set is in "Part I," which focuses on our economic past. The other is in "Part II," which analyzes our current world economy and projects potential future economies, with a focus on moving toward a more cooperative world economy. Some readers may be more interested in "Part I," others in "Part II." It is up to each individual to decide on how they want to approach their reading of the book.

Part I

Our Economic Past

"Part I" provides an overview of the evolution of human economies during the past 300,000 years as well as a comparison with the economies of some of our primate relatives.

One of the most striking facts about our economic past is that more than 95% of it occurred when we were living in small groups of hunters and gatherers. During that time, our economic activities focused primarily on meeting the short-term needs of our families and groups, and their survival from generation to generation.

It wasn't until we settled into a range of different agricultural economies beginning about 12,000 years ago that our lives became much more complex. We established permanent settlements. The size of our population groups grew dramatically and became stratified by wealth and political power. We adopted new technologies at an accelerating rate. Conflict increased, both within and among groups.

Around 5,000 years ago, as our economic activities continued to diversify and political stratification increased, we began a long period of rising and falling empires and long-distance trade in Asia, Europe, Africa, the Americas, and Oceania.

By the end of the 20th century, empires had been replaced by a world of nation-states with very different levels of economic resources and political power.

Chapter 1

You Scratch My Back, Maybe I'll Scratch Yours

Introduction

This chapter provides an overview of chimpanzee economies and makes a comparison with human economies, especially during the time we relied primarily on hunting and gathering for our survival. The purpose of the chapter is to show the surprising similarity, durability, and adaptability of these two sets of economies.

Chimp economies

The description below of the day-to-day lives of chimpanzees in the wild is provided by Project R&R (Release and Restitution for Chimpanzees).[21]

> *"Chimpanzees live, eat, hunt, and play communally in groups. Usually, these groups consist of 20 or 30 individuals but can grow up to several dozen. They call to each other to announce the presence of certain foods or the imminent danger of a predator...*

> *"Chimpanzees learn from each other: how to make a 'night nest' (bed), play, and which plants to eat for medicinal purposes. Through imitation and observation, they learn to make and use tools to crack open nuts, fish insects out of a tree trunk or termite mound, use leaves as sponges, and use objects as weapons. These behaviors are handed down through generations and can vary from one group to another....*

"Chimpanzees search for food communally when foraging or hunting prey. A group of males will chase, corner, and kill small monkeys for meat. Groups sit together for hours, 'fishing' termite mounds or enjoying the ripened fruits of trees."[22]

Chimps, like our own human ancestors, clearly cooperate in the day-to-day activities of living. However, it would be a mistake to look only at the cooperative side of chimp societies and economies. Chimp communities are also hierarchically structured. Violent behavior can occur within groups as well as between them.

Brittany Cohen-Brown wrote an article in The Jane Goodall Institute's newsletter in 2018 in which she discussed the social hierarchy of chimpanzees.[23] *Following are a few excerpts from that article.*

"The highest-ranking chimpanzee in a group is the alpha-male. These males climb their way to the top of the chimpanzee hierarchy, and the ways they choose to do so can differ with the personality of the individual leader. … Below the alpha are several other males with whom the alpha may have complicated relationships. … Females also have a hierarchy within chimpanzee groups, led by the alpha female. … [T]he offspring of higher-ranking females tend to achieve a higher status themselves than chimps born to lower-ranking mothers. … Much of a chimpanzee's life, especially male chimpanzees, is dedicated to climbing up or being knocked down the chimpanzee social ladder."

Hierarchical behavior varies considerably among chimp communities. In some, the dominant males are heavy-handed and violent toward members of their own community as well as highly aggressive toward other chimp groups. In other communities, the behavior of dominant males and females is more benign and based primarily on positive leadership approaches.[24]

As a number of studies have shown, violent behavior by dominant males and others in the group also varies with the environment in which they live. If there is a scarcity of food, neighboring groups of chimps sometimes engage in violent conflict over access to food and territorial boundaries.[25]

Comparison of chimp and human economies

Because chimp economies are partly based on learned behaviors, these primates meet their everyday needs and pass on their survival skills to future generations in ways that vary from group to group. Early human economies probably functioned in very similar ways.[26][27]

A key observation about chimp economies is that joint activities, including hunting, sharing food, and grooming, are not carefully calibrated interactions in which the participants rigorously calculate whether they are getting their fair share of the benefits. The same can be said about many human economic activities. We don't usually ask our partners, "If you do the dishes and pick up the kids after school, and I go grocery shopping and gas up (or charge) the car, who is getting the better deal?"

It's not as if we or chimps never think about fairness in these exchanges. Both species do. There have been some interesting lab experiments in which chimps and other primates have been tested on their sense of fairness. Overall, these experiments show that blatantly biased allocation of rewards does cause unrest among the slighted parties, but that, overall, small imbalances are not a problem.[28]

Thus, many economic activities carried out by humans as well as by chimps are not based on a strictly balanced *quid pro quo*. This is especially true between parents and children, between prime-age adults and the elderly, and between the healthy and the sick or injured.

Diversity of economic relationships

The behavioral examples given above indicate that economic relationships are complex and varied for both humans and our chimp cousins. Following is a list of several kinds of economic interaction that occur among both species:

Habitual economic activities

Both species do things to support the household or the community, or to increase the odds that the group will survive into the next generation without thinking about whether we're getting a fair deal doing them. It's just part of everyday life. This is especially true with childcare. We don't expect our kids to reciprocate all the things we do for them when they are growing up. (That's not to say that we don't expect them to help care for us when they become adults and we become old and less able to meet our own needs.)

Various kinds of reciprocal activities

There are times when we do think about getting a reward or a fair share of something. These kinds of exchange-based activities may vary from a loose sense of fairness to a very rigorous one. The term *barter* is often used when we exchange things or services that we consider to be of approximately equal value.

Command economies

The pattern of powerful individuals or groups ruling the roost is not just a human phenomenon. In addition to the cooperative behavior described above in chimp society, another characteristic is dominance by strong males and females. This type of bully rule very likely goes back to the beginning of our species as well. It certainly characterizes most of recorded human history – for example, the very hierarchical economies of ancient Egypt and Mesoamerica, and many other regional and world empires of the last five millennia. As we all well know, slavery, an extreme form of a command economy, was a basic characteristic of the world's first modern democracy in the United States.

Gifting economies

Giving away food and other resources without the expectation of receiving something in return is also part of chimpanzee and human society. For example, among humans, gifting events – or *potlatches* – were a major economic component of some indigenous tribes in what is now the northwestern United States and southwestern Canada. Local elites would often try to outdo each other in terms of how lavishly they gave things away.[29] It should be noted that there was often a catch to this gift-giving. The givers may not have expected an immediate, reciprocal economic return, but they did expect a return in terms of loyalty and retaining their position of high status within the group.

Economic transactions involving media of exchange

A recent lab-based research project involving the use of tokens rather than food or other direct rewards indicates that non-human primates can grasp the idea of placeholders as a prelude to receiving the reward itself. In other words, humans aren't the only primates able to deal with the abstraction of *media of exchange*. That is, rather than exchanging one desired object for another, the participant is willing to accept something that is not directly valued, but represents a means to acquire a thing of value in the future.[30]

Humans have used cowrie shells, gold nuggets, metal coins, and many other media of exchange to facilitate trade for thousands of years. However, the primate research with tokens described above, and archaeological research on early humans (to be discussed in the next chapter), provide evidence that the use of media of exchange not only goes back to the dawn of our species, but, in terms of cognitive ability, could have been an economic tool for some of our primate ancestors.

Conclusion

The main purpose of this chapter is to show the continuity between non-human primate economies – especially those of our nearest primate relatives, chimpanzees – and our own species. There has been a tendency in the historical and scientific literature to exaggerate the differences between human economies of the past few thousand years and those of our early human ancestors and primate relatives. Recent research, however, indicates that in many basic ways, we survive, adapt, and prepare the way for future generations in much the same manner as we and our relatives have done for hundreds of thousands of years.

We ignore the lessons from these early economies at our own peril. We are currently threatening our own survival and the habitability of our planet in ways that would have been unimaginable to our human and other primate ancestors. In just a few hundred years, we have gone from a mostly sustainable relationship with our environment to one that has brought us to the brink of climate catastrophe.

The next three chapters focus on major economic transitions among humans during the past 300,000 years. During the vast majority of this time, we survived as hunter-gatherers, then gradually shifted to become primarily agriculturalists. The shift from hunting and gathering to the cultivation of plants and animals allowed us to live in more concentrated groups, which, in turn, facilitated more specialized divisions of labor, increased inequalities in wealth and power, accelerated population growth, precipitated more violent conflicts within and between groups, and brought about other changes in our relationships with each other and with the environment.

Chapter 2

The Early Evolution of Human Economies

Introduction

Reviewing much of the current literature on the origins and development of human economies reminds me of the Sunday school classes I reluctantly attended as a child that described the creation of the world. "God did such and such in six days and on the seventh day he rested." Rather than being theocentric, however, these modern-day, "scientific" myths about human economic evolution are heavily biased toward the past 5,000 years or so and on Mesopotamia and the eastern Mediterranean region.

We still have a lot to learn about our hunter-gatherer ancestors. There are many topics on which archaeologists and other scientists disagree about key characteristics of "modern humans" – *Homo sapiens* – between approximately 10,000 and 300,000 years ago. Debates abound about population sizes, migration patterns, when various technologies were developed, relationships between *Homo sapiens* and other human species, and so on.[31] As new archaeological information surfaces and research techniques improve, we will learn much more about our ancestors. In the meantime, we work with what we have.

The primary purpose of this chapter is to provide an overview of the approximately 300,000-year evolution of hunter-gatherer economies across six continents. A secondary purpose is to debunk the ahistorical and geographically-biased views that discount the ingenuity and adaptability of these early humans.

The chapter sets the stage for a better understanding of how human economies have developed, what characterizes them today, and how we might transition to a set of world economies that improves our lives and our environment in the future.

Early economic activities by humans

An article in the March 2018 issue of the Atlantic *reported that: "New finds from Kenya suggest that humans used long-distance trade networks, sophisticated tools, and symbolic pigments right from the dawn of our species."[32]*

The article describes recent finds from an archaeological dig in Kenya suggesting "that human behavior and culture became incredibly sophisticated well before anyone suspected."[33]

"The team found obsidian tools that came from sources dozens of miles away – a sign of long-distance trade networks. They found lumps of black and red rock that had been processed to create pigments – a sign of symbolic thought and representation. They found carefully crafted stone tools. … that are between 305,000 and 320,000 years old.

"Collectively, these finds speak to one of the most important questions in human evolution: When did anatomically modern people, with big brains and bipedal stances, become behaviorally modern, with symbolic art, advanced tools, and a culture that built on itself?"[34]

These findings indicate that this group of humans was far more advanced in their technology and adaptability to changing environmental conditions than scientists would previously have anticipated.

As one archaeologist who was not part of the research team put it: [The results of this project] "provide strong indicators that by about 300,000 years ago we were well on our way to become modern humans in Africa."[35]

A key factor in this research evidence from Kenya is that rapid environmental change – especially the increased frequency of prolonged droughts – played a major role in influencing human behavior to adapt to these new conditions. For example, a drier environment reduced the amount of large game available to the local population. This, in turn, led to the development of more sophisticated hunting and foraging tools and techniques, and to an increase in the range of food-seeking and trading activities (and, more speculatively, a shift to more abstract and symbolic thinking). Adaptation is the key underlying characteristic that allowed our early ancestors to survive in a rapidly changing environment.

Human evolution and migration within and out of Africa

Migration within Africa

Modern humans were the new kids on the block compared to other primate species when we emerged in Africa about 300,000 years ago. Our earliest human ancestors had already been around for about six million years.[36]

By about 200,000 years ago, modern humans had spread throughout most of Africa.[37] Not a lot is known about the reasons for our dispersal across the continent. One of the major causes is likely to have been changes in climate.[38] As the animals we hunted and the plants and seafood we depended on became less available in some areas, we moved to where they were more abundant. (Although the Kenyan example given above indicates that we also improved our hunting and gathering tools and practices to avoid having to relocate.) In addition to climate, another factor that may have contributed to migration was competition for food, particularly with other groups of humans. Of course, these two migratory pushes could have occurred at the same time.

Migration to Asia

Whatever the combination of causes, they also brought about a great migration of modern humans into Asia beginning almost 90,000 years ago[39] – although there is far from universal agreement among scientists about this migration date. It would be wrong to picture this as one large group of migrants trudging northward and eastward together. Rather, what is far more likely is that many small groups of people gradually made their way into southern Asia, with a cumulative large-scale impact over thousands of years.

One can even speculate that there was some back-and-forth movement within this overall migration. Earlier migrants may very well have reported back to later groups in transit or who had not yet begun the trek: "Hey, the hunting and gathering is great up ahead. Come and check it out!"

It is difficult to estimate how many modern humans there were at the time of the "Great Migration." One source estimates that there were about two million modern humans in the world about 50,000 years ago.[40] As the number of human fossil finds increases, and our population estimation techniques improve, these numbers may be revised substantially.

Modern humans, Neanderthals, and Denisovans

Other recent research has caused scientists to rethink previously held views about the relationships between modern humans and other human species. For example, MedlinePlus reports that people of European and Asian descent contain a small percentage of DNA from two other human species – Neanderthals and Denisovans, clearly indicating that we interbred with both of these species.[41]

There is some evidence that the genes from this interbreeding may have increased modern humans' ability to survive in colder climates and/or to fend off various diseases. However, to date, limited research has been done on the effects of these genes on health and other characteristics of modern humans, and are not yet definitive.[42] Stay tuned.

Our migration to Europe

The arrival of modern humans in western Europe was relatively recent – according to one source, about 54,000 years ago.[43] The primary reason for this relatively late migration to Europe appears to have been the cold climate on that continent, including glaciers that last receded about 12,000 years ago.

From Africa to Australia

Migration continued beyond Asia, with one or more groups advancing all the way to Australia about 50,000 years ago.[44] Not unexpectedly, the arrival date of humans in Australia is in dispute among researchers. It seems hard to believe, but it appears that the settling of Australia by aborigines may have occurred not too long after our arrival in western Europe.

> *One plausible route for the trek to Australia begins with early groups of modern humans following the coastlines of Africa, Arabia, India, and Southeast Asia.*
>
> *The next step was probably island hopping from the mainland to New Guinea. At the time of this migration, sea levels were much lower than today, resulting in more land above water and shorter distances between islands. The last leg of the journey, however, from New Guinea to Australia probably entailed almost 100 miles of open sea travel.*
>
> *Research by the Australian Museum concludes that, "The settlement of Australia is the first unequivocal evidence of a major sea crossing, and rates as one of the greatest achievements of early humans."[45]*

From Asia to the Americas

Migration occurred from northeastern Asia to North America primarily via a land bridge across the Bering Sea. The beginning of this migration is estimated to have begun as early as 30,000 years ago.[46] A recent study concludes that modern humans reached southern South America between 18,500 and 15,000 years ago.[47]

Populating the Pacific Islands

Aside from New Guinea and Australia, most of Oceania, including Hawaii and New Zealand, was not populated by humans until the past few thousand to few hundred years ago.[48] As with the migration to Australia, the settling of these islands was a remarkable feat. Imagine these ancient mariners traveling hundreds, or, in a few cases, over a thousand miles across ocean waters with no land in sight.

Implications of early hunter-gatherer economies for human economies today

Just as the world was not created in seven days, the economic activities of humans did not suddenly become "modern" 5,000 years ago. Complex human economies began in Africa more than 300,000 years ago.

Modern humans migrated, interbred, and adapted to changing environmental conditions in Africa for more than 200,000 years before significant numbers of us moved northward and eastward into Asia beginning almost 90,000 years ago. This migration was probably primarily a result of increasingly dry conditions in northeastern Africa.

What this overview of the evolution and growth of Homo sapiens tells us is that humans were incredibly resourceful and adaptable right from the time of our emergence as a species. All of the 20 or so other human species[49] have become extinct, very probably because of their inability to adapt to changing environmental conditions, and, possibly, because they were out-competed and/or "out-cooperated" by modern humans when economic resources became scarce.

During this immense period of time, our ancestors were able to develop and modify hundreds of thousands of different local economies in environments ranging from extreme heat to extreme cold and from prolonged droughts to long periods of high rainfall – in some cases having to make rapid adjustments to their economies when local conditions changed abruptly.

The next chapter focuses on a major transformation of our economic lives from being primarily dependent on hunting and gathering activities for our survival to primarily basing our livelihood on the cultivation of plants and animals.

Chapter 3

The Emergence of Agricultural Economies

The following story from a 2016 article in *The New York Times*, unveils an early agricultural community.

> *"Beneath a rocky slope in central Jordan lie the remains of a 10,000-year-old village called Ain Ghazal, whose inhabitants lived in stone houses with timber roof beams, the walls and floors gleaming with white plaster. … [It was] one of the first farming villages to have emerged after the dawn of agriculture.*
>
> *"Around the settlement, Ain Ghazal farmers raised barley, wheat, chickpeas, and lentils. Other villagers would leave for months at a time to herd sheep and goats in the surrounding hills.*
>
> *"Sites like Ain Ghazal provide a glimpse of one of the most important transitions in human history: the moment that people domesticated plants and animals, settled down, and began to produce the kind of society in which most of us live today."*[50]

As discussed in the previous chapter, modern humans began their existence as a species about 300,000 years ago. Between 12,000 and 5,000 years ago, different groups underwent shifts from hunter-gatherer economies to economic systems based on growing crops and domesticating animals.

This chapter explores where and why this momentous economic transition began and what its implications have been for subsequent generations, in particular for the types of economies that grew out of this transition.

Different paths from hunting and gathering to farming

Most scientists who study prehistoric agriculture agree that multiple independent agricultural revolutions took place in different parts of the world.[51] One generalized factor that appears to have set the stage for these disparate agricultural revolutions was the end of the last Ice Age around 12,000 years ago. This global climate event not only created warmer temperatures but also periodic droughts, and significant changes in flora and fauna. In many instances, these changes made agriculture more attractive because groups of humans could increase their food security by raising crops and animals instead of by foraging and hunting for food.

In addition to changing environments, another factor in our transition to agriculture was the development of tools that made farming easier. For the most part, we used a range of increasingly sophisticated stone tools up to about 5,000 years ago.

Then came the Bronze Age that lasted from about 5,000 to a little over 3,000 years ago. During this period, we learned to make bronze out of copper and tin. This metal alloy was "used for weapons and tools. … [T]he harder metal replaced its stone predecessors and helped spark innovations including the ox-drawn plow and the wheel."[52]

During the next 2,000 years or so, we learned ways to heat and forge iron. "At the time, the metal was seen as more precious than gold, and wrought iron (which would be replaced by steel with the advent of smelting iron) was easier to manufacture than bronze." The use of iron tools such as sickles and plowshares greatly increased the productivity of agriculture.[53] Iron and steel weapons such as "swords, spears, lances, axes and arrowheads"[54] also increased our ability to hunt and kill animals, including each other.

There are two important caveats to the argument for a post-Ice Age transition to agriculture. Some archaeological evidence points to a long, gradual transition from hunting and gathering to agriculture rather than to a number of abrupt changes in the last dozen or so millennia. For example, research in Mozambique indicates that humans collected, stored, and consumed sorghum grains more than 100,000 years ago.[55] Other research indicates that early humans practiced forest and other landscape management techniques for thousands of years before the "agricultural revolution," including controlled burns and forest gardening, to increase the availability of desirable animals and plants.[56]

The second caveat is that hunting and gathering activities are still part of our world economy today. Fishing may be the most prominent example, but we also cut down trees for a variety of human uses, hunt deer, seals, and other animals, and collect wild mushrooms and other plants. Some cultures around the world are still primarily dependent on hunting and gathering for their livelihoods.

The emergence of agriculture economies around the world

Before we get too far into a discussion of why humans became farmers and what that means for us today, here is a brief description of the major locations in which agriculture began between 12 and two millennia ago.

The emergence of agriculture has been place- and time-specific, and has had major consequences for patterns of local and regional economic development (and stagnation), and for the ability of some groups of humans to dominate other groups.

The Fertile Crescent

Scientists tell us that the first humans to make a major transition to agriculture was about 12,000 years ago among people who resided in the Fertile Crescent – a region that encompasses modern Iraq, Syria, Lebanon, Palestine, Israel, Jordan, and northern Egypt. The village of Ain Ghazal, mentioned above, is located in this area near present-day Amman, Jordan. In addition to productive soils and favorable growing conditions after the last Ice Age, this region also featured the Tigris, Euphrates, and Nile rivers, all excellent sources of irrigation.

According to encyclopedia.com, "The region was home to a variety of edible and easily cultivated crops: wheat and barley among the cereal crops, and lentils, peas, and chickpeas among the vegetables. Also, the region was endowed with wild goats, sheep, pigs, and cattle, all of which were domesticated and became important sources of food. Cattle are also useful work animals, and all these animals produce manure for fertilizer. Thus, a complete agricultural package was available."[57]

Not only is the Fertile Crescent considered by most researchers to be the place where agriculture first emerged, it was also the source from which farming spread to other parts of East Asia, Europe, and northern Africa during the next several millennia.

China

China appears to have been the home of two separate agricultural revolutions – one in the north and one in the south.

A *Year of China* article posted online by Brown University reports that, "The transition from hunting and gathering to cultivation of wild plants was initiated by semi-sedentary communities some 11,000 years ago. Among the earliest East Asian pioneering foragers were those who lived in North China who started cultivating wild millet. Within one or two millennia, the annually cultivated millet became domesticated and was joined by corralling and eventual domestication of pigs. Stable food production and storage allowed for a rapid demographic increase and the spread of villages to the periphery of the core area."[58]

Agriculture emerged 1,000 to 2,000 years later in South China. This delay is attributed by some scientists to the greater availability of game and forageable food in the south compared to the north. As a result, there was not as much pressure in the south to become farmers. The big breakthrough crop in the south was the cultivation of rice.

South Asia

The earliest agriculture in South Asia appears to have been along the western tributaries of the Indus River (in present-day Pakistan) between 8,000 and 11,000 years ago. Crops included barley and wheat. Sheep, goats, and cattle were domesticated at about the same time.[59]

Central Eurasia

Archaeological evidence indicates that the domestication of horses took place about 6,000 years ago in the steppe lands north of the Black Sea from Ukraine to Kazakhstan.[60] As we shall see in the next chapter, horses were not just farm animals. They played a major role in revolutionizing the transportation of goods and people, and as a means of waging war all the way up to the beginning of the 20th century.[61]

Papua New Guinea

Agriculture began in Papua New Guinea between 7,000 and 10,000 years ago. Crops included taro, bananas, and yams.[62]

The Americas

Agriculture began independently in three areas of the Americas – with sites in South America and Mexico (Mesoamerica) dating back to 8,000 to 9,000 years ago, and sites in eastern North America beginning between 4,000 and 5,000 years ago. Peanuts, squash, and potatoes were early crops grown in South America. Llamas and alpacas were the primary animals domesticated. In Mesoamerica, squash and maize were cultivated, and turkeys were domesticated. Early crops in North America included squash and sunflowers.[63] [64]

West Africa

Farming began independently in West Africa about 5,000 years ago. Early crops included sorghum and oil palm.[65]

Australia

Archaeological research indicates that Aborigines began farming more than 2,000 years ago.[66] "Aboriginal people grew. ... yams,. ... native millet, macadamia nuts, fruits and berries. [They also] reared dingoes, possums, emus and cassowaries, moved caterpillars to new breeding areas and carried fish stock across country."[67]

Major takeaways from these regional agricultural revolutions

There appear to have been a number of interconnected factors affecting the transition among different groups of humans from hunting and gathering economies to agricultural economies beginning about 12 millennia ago: a warming climate, more frequent drought conditions, fewer animals to hunt and/or plants to gather, the increasing availability of plants and animals well-suited to domestication, access to reliable sources of water, fertile soils, improved tools, and increasing population density.

These groups of humans adopted different combinations of environmental, social, and technological practices that affected when and how their local economies evolved. The common denominator is that many of these groups were able to develop means for surviving and reproducing in their specific circumstances.

Throughout prior human history, negative changes in local environments often led groups to migrate to other locations – in general, following the game and/or seeking out better sources of forageable food and water. In some cases, groups stayed in their local areas and made changes in their hunting and gathering practices in order to survive. There is a third option as well – the dying out of a group or, in extreme cases, an entire species of our human cousins, because of bad choices, bad luck, or insurmountable obstacles to survival.[68]

By about 10,000 years ago, modern humans had spread across most of the habitable world and, thus, had fewer places to migrate to. Changing the ways they met their food and other survival needs required a different type of economic adaptation – increasing the availability of animals and other food rather than going elsewhere to find them. Those humans who succeeded in increasing the availability of food and other means of survival, without having to move, began to dominate our species. Those who were hunter-gatherers continued to live on parts of the planet that could sustain this style of life, but they became a distinct minority.

Thus, by about 5,000 years ago, most humans had developed local economies that were primarily dependent on cultivated plants and domesticated animals. This transition entailed a radical change in the way people led their day-to-day lives. Most of them began to live in permanent or semi-permanent villages rather than being primarily nomadic or semi-nomadic. By growing plants and animals, and storing food, they created greater security against drought and other threats to their food supply. This approach to survival led to an increase in population. But the combination of permanent or semi-permanent communities and population growth was a recipe for conflict within and among these groups and between them and nomadic groups. It also led to increasingly hierarchical structures within these societies. For the first time, the local economies of our species came into long-term conflict with one another, which in one way or another has continued to the present time.

There is another type of conflict – between humans and the physical environment – that was exacerbated by the development of agricultural economies. Humans began to radically alter their physical environments in order to make way for cultivated plants and concentrations of grazing animals. Aside from occasional over-harvesting of wild plants and animals by hunter-gatherers, humans had played a relatively benign role in their relationship with nature since the beginning of the species. The shift to agriculture set the stage for a major and increasingly disruptive impact by humans on the environment, one which has reached a critical level in the early 21st century.

In the next chapter, we will explore ways in which human economies grew in size, and increasingly came into conflict with one another and with Mother Nature during the past 5,000 years.

Chapter 4

Five Millennia of Political and Economic Chaos

Introduction

The age of increasingly turbulent economies began about 5,000 years ago. As agricultural techniques improved, farmers produced greater surpluses that could support more non-farming activities. The size and density of population centers grew. Economic inequality increased as some members of society began to specialize in work other than farming or became political, economic, and/or religious elites. Also, with urban population growth, the potential for conflict increased – both within these settlements and between them and other groups of humans. As cultivated and grazing areas displaced forests and grasslands, and as population centers grew in size, humans had a greater negative impact on the environment.[69]

From villages to cities to city-states to empires

For about 300,000 years, the number of modern humans who lived as hunter-gatherers was relatively static or increased very gradually.[70] [71] [72] [73]

It was only once some of us established semi-permanent and permanent settlements that our population increased significantly. Why was this? Primarily because we increased the reliability of our food supply through growing and raising it ourselves rather than facing the uncertainties of going out and having to find it in the wild.

But population growth came at a price. As groups became bigger, small collections of huts became villages. Many villages became small cities, then larger cities, then clusters of cities. These larger population groups were more likely to experience internal conflicts and economic inequality. They also became targets for outsiders who saw the potential for easy pickings. Why grow or hunt your own food and other goods when you can plunder your neighbors'?

The following examples of ancient population centers, all in Mesopotamia, illustrate both the benefits and the plights of these early, expanding economies.

The emergence of cities

An article by Colin Renfrew published in a 2006 edition of *Human Paleontology and Prehistory* provides a glimpse of life in one of the oldest cities discovered by archaeologists.

Çatalhöyük

"Çatalhöyük. … located in what is now south-central Turkey,. … was founded about 9,000 years ago and abandoned about 1,400 years later. Its peak population appears to have been around 10,000 inhabitants. The small city's economy was based on a combination of hunting and raising plants and animals. The residents were also involved in pottery making, the manufacture of obsidian tools, mining and smelting of lead, and trade (for example, exchanging obsidian tools with groups in Syria for shells and flint).

"Çatalhöyük has strong evidence of [having been] an egalitarian society, as no houses with distinctive features (belonging to royalty or religious hierarchy, for example) have been found so far. The most recent investigations also reveal little social distinction based on gender, with men and women

receiving equivalent nutrition and seeming to have equal social status..."[74]

"We believe that environmental degradation and climate change forced community members to move further away from the settlement to farm and to find supplies like firewood. ... That contributed to the ultimate demise of Çatalhöyük."[75]

Bickering among city-states

City-states emerged as agricultural communities grew and expanded into clusters of communities. Probably the best known of these clusters are the city-states of ancient Greece, especially the rivalry between Athens and Sparta. According to *National Geographic,* there were more than 1,000 of these city-states spread across what is now modern Greece.[76] They emerged over 5,000 years ago and lasted for more than 2,000 years.[77] These communities often developed in rugged landscapes and with distances among them that were conducive to divergent local societies, political structures, and economies. As a result, they didn't always play well together. Below is the story of one of the first clusters of city-states to emerge in the world.

Sumeria

An article by Joshua Mark in the World Historical Encyclopedia *provides an overview of the relationship among Sumeria's city-states. There were about a dozen of them in what is now south-central Iraq. They came into existence about 6,400 years ago and lasted for about 2,400 years. At its peak, the largest city-state may have had up to 80,000 residents. The city-states shared a common language and culture, but the relationships among them were very contentious. Archaeological and written evidence (some of it in Sumerian, the first known written language, which emerged about 5,400 years ago) indicates that the city-states were often at war with one another, trading off periodically in terms of which one dominated the rest.*[78]

Mark writes that, "Since their homeland was largely devoid of timber, stone and minerals, the Sumerians were forced to create one of history's earliest trade networks over both land and sea. Their most important commercial partner may have been the island of Dilmun (present day Bahrain), which held a monopoly on the copper trade, but their merchants also undertook months-long journeys to Anatolia and Lebanon to gather cedar wood and to Oman and the Indus Valley for gold and gemstones..."[79]

The lack of cohesion among the city-states appears to have been a key factor in the demise of Sumeria. It came under the control of the Akkadian empire more than 4,000 years ago.[80]

The beginning of Empires

As shown in both Greece and Sumeria, city-states were inherently unstable, both because of internal rivalries and also threats from outsiders. As a result, during most of the past 5,000 years, empires became a predominant form of human organization in which centralized leadership replaced the more amorphous and disparate structures of city-states. One of the earliest empires is described below.

Akkadia

According to some historians, "Akkadia was the world's first empire. It was established in Mesopotamia around 4,300 years ago after its ruler, Sargon of Akkad, united a series of independent city-states. Akkadian influence spanned along the Tigris and Euphrates rivers from what is now southern Iraq, through to Syria and Turkey.[81]

"Sumer and Akkad had a surplus of agricultural products but was short of almost everything else, particularly metal ores, timber, and building stone, all of which had to be imported."[82]

"Trade extended from the silver mines of Anatolia to the lapis lazuli mines in modern Afghanistan, the cedars of Lebanon and the copper of Magan. This consolidation of the city-states of Sumer and Akkad reflected the growing economic and political power of Mesopotamia. The empire's breadbasket was the rain-fed agricultural system and a chain of fortresses was built to control the imperial wheat production."[83]

"Then, about a century after its formation, the Akkadian Empire suddenly collapsed, followed by mass migration and conflicts...[84] *A recent study has identified "two major drought periods which started 4,510 and 4,260 years ago, and lasted 110 and 290 years respectively. The latter event occurs precisely at the time of the Akkadian Empire's collapse and provides a strong argument that climate change was at least in part responsible."*[85]

Empires and trade all over the world

Akkadia may have been the first empire in the world, but it was one of hundreds that rose and fell on five continents during the past five millennia. Not only did these empires create regional groupings of multiple states under the control of one ruler or government,[86] they also radically altered human economies by facilitating long-distance trade with other empires and with other groups of humans throughout the world.

There are a variety of causes for the emergence and decline of these empires. It makes sense that many of them developed in the same geographical areas in which humans first began farming. As mentioned above, agriculture set the stage for diversified economies. Empires were regional and political manifestations of that economic diversification. Following are a few major examples of these empires, the trade relationships they developed, and reasons for their demise.

The Middle East and Mediterranean Sea

As the examples presented above indicate, the Fertile Crescent not only experienced one of the earliest transitions to agriculture but also to major human settlements and centers of long-distance trade. Egypt, on the edge of the Fertile Crescent, developed one of the first kingdoms in the world about five millennia ago. This is not surprising due to its location on the Nile River and the Mediterranean Sea, conducive to irrigated agriculture, urbanization, and long-distance trade.

It is also not surprising that two great civilizations emerged almost 3,000 years ago in nearby Greece and Italy along the Mediterranean Sea. Although not among the first farmers in the world, Greeks and Romans were among the early adopters of agricultural practices, because of their proximity to the Fertile Crescent. In addition, their access to the sea greatly facilitated their involvement in early long-distance trade.

At its peak, almost 2,000 years ago, the Roman Empire covered virtually all of Europe, a good part of Western Asia, and the northern edge of Africa,[87] not only subjugating almost 60 million people, but also expanding agriculture and trade throughout much of this vast region.[88]

China

China has spawned more than a dozen empires in the past 4,000 years, beginning with the Xia Dynasty and culminating in the current People's Republic of China. The country occupies a little over 6% of the world's total land mass and almost 18% of its population. Beginning with the start-up of the "Silk Road" about

2,400 years ago, China has been involved in widespread international trade.[89]

South Asia

South Asia, primarily comprised of contemporary India and Pakistan, has seen more than a dozen empires come and go. For example, the Mauryan Empire originated in eastern India about 2,300 years ago, lasted more than 100 years, and was the first empire to occupy most of the Indian subcontinent.[90] The subcontinent's international trade was strongly impacted by several of the routes referred to as the Silk Road.[91]

Southeast Asia

Depending on who is doing the counting, modern Southeast Asia[92] consists of 11 to 13 countries with a total population of almost 700 million.[93] Indonesia is the most populous with more than 270 million inhabitants (the fourth-largest country in the world). Brunei is the smallest with fewer than a half-million people. Beginning about 1,300 years ago, at least ten kingdoms rose and fell in different parts of Southeast Asia. There were Hindu, Buddhist, and Muslim kingdoms in various parts of the region. The most recent of these kingdoms kept European imperial powers from colonizing Thailand until the end of the 19th century.[94]

Sub-Saharan Africa

The largest and most powerful sub-Saharan African empire was the Songhai Empire. It began about 1,200 years ago and lasted for almost 600 years. Timbuktu, a pivotal city in the empire, played a major role in caravan trade across the Sahara Desert.[95] The predominant items traded north were gold, salt, ivory, cloth, and slaves. Horses, books, and metal goods (including weapons) were major items traded south.[96]

The Mongol Empire

As mentioned in the previous chapter, the domestication of the horse began in the steppe lands north of the Black Sea about 6,000 years ago, but the Mongols to the east of this region became the preeminent horse culture in the world, most notably during the Mongol Empire under Genghis Khan and his heirs about 1,000 years ago. The Mongols' expert use of mounted cavalry allowed them to gain control over about nine million square miles of land in Asia and eastern Europe. This was the fifth-largest geographical area under one rule in human history. (The Soviet Union/Russia was and is the largest, followed by the British empire in the early 20th century. Canada is next, followed closely by the United States and modern China.) The brutal campaigns of the Mongol empire caused approximately 40 million deaths, about 11% of the world's estimated population at that time. The Mongols were much better at conquering lands than governing them, thus the short duration of about 100 years of their empire.[97][98]

Papua New Guinea

As discussed in the previous chapter, the inhabitants of Papua New Guinea began to farm between 10,000 and 7,000 years ago,[99] but unlike in Eurasia, North Africa, and parts of the Americas, agriculture did not lead to empire-building. A couple of likely reasons for this are the mountainous terrain of the islands and the large number of ethnic groups that made consolidation into large political units difficult.[100] Over the millennia, the inhabitants of Papua New Guinea have engaged in both trade and conflict. Most historical trade was in food, tools, weapons, and pottery among different groups in the islands.[101] Much of the historical conflict involved ritualized fighting that resulted in limited loss of life. However, with the advent of modern weaponry and the breakdown of some traditional norms, intergroup conflict has become much more deadly in recent years.[102]

The Americas

There were several ancient civilizations in the Americas, most notably Norte Chico which began about 5,000 years ago on the coastal plains of Peru;[103] the Mayan Empire in Central America which began more than 1,000 years ago and ended before the arrival of the Europeans; and the Incan Empire in the Andes region and the Aztec Empire in Mexico, both of which began within the last thousand years and were destroyed by the Spanish in the 1500s.[104] Little is known about trade in Norte Chico, but long-distance exchange was a thriving part of the economies of the later empires of South and Central America.[105]

Although farming was practiced in eastern North America beginning about 5,000 years ago[106], there have been no North American empires. The city of Cahokia was a major trade center on the Mississippi River near what is now St. Louis and had as many as 20,000 inhabitants about 1,000 years ago.[107] But it was not the center of an empire. North America had hundreds of separate ethnic and language groups who traded and periodically fought with one another, but none established a long-term dominant position over the others.[108]

Australia

Before the British arrived in Australia in the late 1700s,[109] the Aborigines were primarily hunters and gatherers with only limited involvement in farming. Relatively minor skirmishing occurred among different groups. However, there don't appear to have been any large-scale conflicts.[110] There was long-distance trading, including items such as ochres (for painting), stone axes, and boomerangs.[111]

Dramatic changes in the world's economies began about 700 years ago

European empires conquered the rest of the world

There was a major change in the structure of empires and trade beginning in the 1400s. Up until that time, the large majority of empires came and went by subjugating nearby regions and then falling into decline for a variety of reasons, including conquest by other empires, internal governance or succession problems, disease (for example, the black plague in Europe in the 1300s killed almost a third of the continent's population),[112] [113] or dramatic climate changes, especially extended droughts.

Trade generally occurred on a somewhat parallel track to each empire's pattern of conquest and governance. Some examples are the east-west trade routes between Asia and Europe including various versions of the Silk Road, trans-Saharan caravans linking the Middle East and sub-Saharan Africa, networks of Roman roads connecting southern and northern Europe, and north-south land and water routes in the Americas.

Then Henry the Navigator, a member of the Portuguese royal family, played a lead role in changing the patterns of trade and conquest beginning in the early 1400s. Although a small country, Portugal became a maritime power with its exploration along the coast of Africa, its circumnavigation of that continent, and its direct maritime trade with Asia.[114]

King Ferdinand and Queen Isabella of Spain followed suit in the latter part of the 1400s by strengthening their country's maritime fleet and using it for long-distance trade and conquest, including Columbus' "discovery" of the Americas in 1492, and Spain's subsequent colonization of most of Central and South America during the next three centuries.[115]

The emergence of royally approved joint-stock companies

Around 1600, the Dutch and the English initiated a new phase of this European, maritime-based empire-building by developing royally approved trading companies that allowed for private shareholder investments.[116] The Dutch East India Company and the (British) East India Company were established as joint-stock corporations. They became two of the largest companies the world has ever seen.

The French, Belgians, and Germans joined the fray, and by the end of the late 1700s, the European empires had used their naval and military superiority to carve up the world into regions designed to colonize foreign lands and their people for the purpose of enriching European royal families and private investors.

As noted above, royally sanctioned, for-profit corporations played a critical role in this European expansion. Although often referred to as "trading" companies, they were often far more than that. The largest of these corporations were also "surrogate" government entities that administered and had military control over large geographical areas and population groups as well as playing the role of traders and, sometimes, expropriators of goods and services.

The (British) East India Company (EIC)

The company "was an English, and later British, joint-stock company founded in 1600. It was formed to trade in the Indian Ocean region, initially with the East Indies (the Indian subcontinent and Southeast Asia), and later with East Asia. The company seized control of large parts of the Indian subcontinent, colonised parts of Southeast Asia and Hong Kong, and kept trading posts and colonies in the Persian Gulf Residencies. At its peak, the company was the largest corporation in the world. The EIC had its own armed forces in the form of the company's three Presidency armies, totaling about 260,000 soldiers, twice the size of the army of Britain [at that time]. The operations of the company had a profound effect on the global balance of trade."[117]

From mercantilism to the industrial revolution

The radical changes in the world political and economic order wrought by the European empires and their for-profit affiliates were not just limited to trade and colonization. They had an enormous technological component as well, often referred to as The Industrial Revolution, that continues into the 21st century.

To quote from a Wikipedia article: "The Industrial Revolution was a period of global transition of human economy towards more efficient and stable manufacturing processes that succeeded the Agricultural Revolution, starting from Great Britain, continental Europe, and the United States, that occurred during the period from around 1760 to about 1820–1840. This transition included going from hand production methods to machines; new chemical manufacturing and iron production processes; the increasing use of water power and steam power; the development of machine tools; and the rise of the mechanized factory system. Output greatly increased, and a result was an unprecedented rise in population and in the rate of population growth. The textile industry was the first to use modern production methods, and textiles became the dominant industry in terms of employment, value of output, and capital invested…

"The Industrial Revolution marked a major turning point in history. Comparable only to humanity's adoption of agriculture with respect to material advancement, the Industrial Revolution influenced in some way almost every aspect of daily life. In particular, average income and population began to exhibit unprecedented sustained growth…"[118]

As we shall see in "Part II" of the book, the Industrial Revolution also had major long-term, negative impacts[119] – including urban overcrowding, poor health and working conditions, pollution, the exacerbation of inequalities within and among countries, and the unsustainable warming of the planet due to exponential increases in fossil fuel emissions.

The demise of European empires from the late 18th through the 20th centuries
This Eurocentric division of the world was relatively short-lived compared to many empires during the previous few thousand years. This was primarily because of in-fighting among the European empires, the rebellion of colonists and the colonized, and the difficulty of managing far-flung empires.

These modern European empires began to crumble with the successful American War of Independence in the late 1700s, followed by wars of liberation in Latin America in the early 1800s, and conflicts among European powers.

Thus, the European conquest of the world, joined by the United States after independence, did not engender a successful, long-term economic development model, and was dismantled in the 1900s through two world wars, a world depression, and political dissension in many parts of the colonized world.

The Second World War was the final straw that broke the back of this imperial model of development and put the world on course to be divided up among "independent" nation-states.

From empires to neocolonialism
A major qualification to this demise of European empires (and the quasi-empire formed by the United States) is that many of the countries liberated in the 19th and 20th centuries continued to be heavily dependent – economically and politically – on their former imperial rulers and/or other powerful nation-states.

The most powerful of these neocolonial countries was, and is, the United States. The country was originally comprised of 13 former British colonies on the eastern edge of North America with a combined population of about 2.5 million and a land area of less than 500,000 square miles.[120] As the United States expanded west during the following 200+ years, it has grown to more than 330 million people and almost four million square miles.[121] [122] [123]

It is important to note that the original colonies themselves were comprised of land formally inhabited by Native Americans, as was the approximately 3.5 million square miles added after independence. An exception to this usurpation of Native American lands was the annexation of land previously controlled by the Spanish in the southwest and most of California in which the subjugation of the indigenous population had already been long underway.

The size of the United States described above represents only the country's 50 states. In addition, the U.S. has strong political, economic, and military influence over its neighbors in the Caribbean, and Central and South America, as well as in countries and territories in other parts of the world. It continues to be the dominant world power in the early 21st-century (with China looming not far behind).

General Smedley Butler, a highly decorated Marine officer in the first quarter of the 20th century, reflected on his military role on behalf of the United States:

> *"I was a racketeer, a gangster for capitalism. I suspected I was just part of a racket at the time. Now I am sure of it. ... I helped make Mexico, especially Tampico, safe for American oil interests in 1914. I helped make Haiti and Cuba a decent place for the National City Bank boys to collect revenues in. I helped in the raping of half a dozen Central American republics for the benefits of Wall Street ... Looking back on it, I feel that I could have given Al Capone a few hints. The best he could do*

was to operate his racket in three districts. I operated on three continents."[124]

Of course, the United States is only one prominent example of neocolonialism. Former European empires as well as other politically and economically dominant countries – including China and Russia – continue to play the role of neocolonialists to less well-off nation-states around the world.

A new era in the last half of the 20th century

The United Nations was formed about six weeks after the end of World War II in October 1945 with 51 original member-states. Beginning with the independence of Indonesia in 1945 and India and Pakistan in 1947, former colonies all over the world became independent countries, primarily in the 1950s through the 1970s. The dissolutions of the Soviet Union and Yugoslavia in 1991 and 1992 added to the number of these nation-states. There were 193 member-countries of the United Nations in 2023. Thus, the number of UN members almost quadrupled since the end of the Second World War. This change represents a dramatic shift from a world comprised of empires and subjugated peoples to a world organized as a group of nation-states. However, as stated above, it is important to keep in mind that most of the newly established, independent nation-states continued to be economically and politically dominated by of the world's most powerful countries.

Conclusion

After 300,000 years or so, humans had populated virtually all of the habitable parts of the planet. This human growth and dispersal was a very long and often messy process. Our gradual migration as hunter-gatherers out of *Africa* to the other five habitable continents beginning almost 90,000 years ago probably did not involve much conflict and fighting over territory. But as we shifted to agricultural economies and developed permanent settlements, our population groups became increasingly large and stratified. We became more likely to fight with one another, not only between groups but within communities. Our villages became cities, then city-states and empires. We experienced about 5,000 years of bloody conflicts to divvy up the planet and its resources.

For most of the past 700 years, a small number of seafaring European empires dominated the world's political and economic scene. During the 20th century, this domination was undercut by two world wars and the Great Depression. As a result, the world became divided up into about 200 countries rather than a small group of colonizers and a large group of subjugated regions.

However, the colonial relations of the past continue to the present day in the form of neocolonialism in which many of these new nation-states are at the political and economic mercy of a small number of dominant countries.

The main intent of the formation of the United Nations in 1945 was to establish a world of independent nation-states, and alliances among them, as the primary means to reduce the odds of large-scale economic crises and political conflicts. However, attempts at increasing political harmony and decreasing conflict and economic instability have had mixed results since 1945.

"Part II, Toward a Cooperative World Economy," the second section of this book, begins with a chapter that defines useful and not-so-useful concepts related to the world's recent and current economic problems and potential solutions. It then provides an analysis of the major ways in which our world of mixed economies is falling short in terms of creating democracy, economic justice, political stability, and environmental sustainability. The primary focus of the seven chapters of "Part II" is on how we can make the transition to a more cooperative economy that creates a better life for all of us and for the other species on our planet during the next quarter century and beyond.

Part II

Toward a Cooperative World Economy

"Part I" of this book provided an overview of the evolution of human economies during the past 300,000 years (as well as a comparison with the economies of some of our primate relatives). One of the most striking things about our economic past is that the vast majority of it occurred when we were living in small groups of hunters and gatherers. During that time, our economic activities focused primarily on meeting the short-term survival needs of our families and groups and continuing to survive from generation to generation.

It wasn't until we settled into a range of different agricultural economies beginning about 12,000 years ago that our lives became much more complex. We established permanent settlements. The size of our population groups grew dramatically and became stratified by wealth and political power. Conflict increased, both within and among groups.

Around 5,000 years ago, as our economic activities continued to diversify and political stratification increased, we began a long period of rising and falling empires and long-distance trade in Asia, Europe, Africa, the Americas, and Oceania. By the end of the 20th century, empires had been replaced by a world of nation-states with very different levels of economic resources and political power.

Chapter 5, the first chapter in "Part II," examines the ways in which we are falling short in the early decades of this century in addressing the four major components of a more cooperative world economy: political democracy, economic democracy, quality of life, and environmental sustainability.

This sobering assessment is followed by five chapters that present recommendations and strategies for intergovernmental organizations, countries, businesses, nonprofit organizations, and local and global initiatives to address these four components of a more cooperative economy. The book concludes with a comprehensive, measurable approach to bring about a more cooperative world economy by 2050.

Major Problems in Our Current World of Mixed Economies

Introduction

At the beginning of the 21st century (about 300,000 years after the emergence of our species), some of us thought that we had finally developed a strategy for world peace and prosperity. Almost 200 nation-states had become members of the United Nations; the UN had launched its Millennium Development Goals program in 2000, in which world leaders committed "to combat poverty, hunger, disease, illiteracy, environmental degradation, and discrimination against women."[125]; and almost all of the countries of the world had become interlinked by a variety of economic and political institutions and agreements.

Unfortunately, it turns out that we had, and still have, a long way to go to create world peace, shared prosperity, and a sustainable environment.

This chapter starts with a set of definitions of useful and not-so-useful terms that may help our understanding of the world's major economic problems. The chapter then summarizes these problems that continue to plague the world.

Definitions related to the contemporary world's economies

One of my sociology professors once said, "Social theories are not right or wrong, they are either useful or not." I have come to apply this distinction to social, political, and economic concepts and strategies as well as to social theories.

Following are five concepts that I put into the "not useful" category:

Capitalism

The online version of the *Oxford English Dictionary* defines capitalism as "an economic and political system in which a country's trade and industry are controlled by private owners for profit, rather than by the state."[126]

The uselessness of this definition is based on the fact that there is not now, nor has there ever been, such a system. In every real-world country, private "trade and industry" have always been regulated, taxed, and in other ways overseen by the state. To be sure, the degree of government involvement in the economy has varied dramatically by country, but it has always been there.

Homo economicus

Homo economicus (economic man) is a sister concept to capitalism that is equally not useful. By one definition, it portrays humans as "agents who are consistently rational and narrowly self-interested, and who pursue their subjectively defined ends optimally."[127]

Economic man is another canard used by some economists to pigeonhole humans as a species that is wholly consumed with selfishness. This characterization is neither accurate nor useful. We humans have many other characteristics that motivate us besides greed.

Liberalism

As defined by Wikipedia, "Liberalism is a political and moral philosophy based on the rights of the individual, liberty, consent of the governed, political equality, right to private property and equality before the law. Liberals espouse various views depending on their understanding of these principles, but generally support private property, market economies, individual rights (including civil rights and human rights), liberal democracy, secularism, rule of law, economic and political freedom, freedom of speech, freedom of the press, freedom of assembly, and freedom of religion, constitutional government and privacy rights. Liberalism is frequently cited as the dominant ideology of modern history."[128]

As the above citation states, "Liberals espouse various views depending on their understanding of ['liberal'] principles." This diversity of views results in a hodgepodge of different meanings and the relative importance of individual rights, liberty, and other values. These issues are important topics of debate and discussion, but they don't constitute an easily measurable component of a specific kind of economy, let alone what constitutes a cooperative economy.

Socialism

One basic definition of socialism is that "the means of production are owned by the state."[129] This oversimplification of the control of the economy is on the opposite end of the spectrum from the definition of capitalism given above. There is no state in history that has achieved total control over the economy. Even North Korea has strong and growing private sector economic activity.[130]

Communism

There are two prominent definitions of communism:
1. "An economic system in which the state controls the means of producing everything on behalf of the people."[131]
2. "A classless societal system in which property and wealth [are] distributed equally and without the need for a coercive government."[132]

These radically divergent definitions make this concept useless. Stalin's mass murder of 20 million or more Russians and Mao's starvation of about the same number of Chinese citizens are not the same "communism" as a classless society of self-governed people.[133]

The shortcomings of all of the above concepts can drive flawed and destructive economic policies.

Useful concepts

As presented briefly in the book's introduction, the following concepts, in contrast, are useful in understanding and analyzing past, current and potential human economies.

Mixed economy

A mixed economy is "an economy with a mixture of state and private enterprises. Some economic activities are carried out by individuals or firms taking independent economic decisions, coordinated by markets; others are carried on by organizations under state ownership and control, with some degree of centralized decision-taking. Most actual economies are mixed, in the sense of having substantial elements of both forms of economic organization."[134]

The phrase mixed economy – "an economic system combining private and public enterprise" – is far more useful in describing the range of economic relationships between private enterprises and the state than are the "useless" concepts presented above.

Note that mixed economies occur at different levels in society. Local, regional, national, and international economies vary, sometimes dramatically, including among regions within the same country. They also vary in terms of being located at different points along a continuum from a relatively high degree of market-based decision-making by private enterprises to a high degree of state decision-making and control. It is also noteworthy that within the same locality, region, nation, or group of nations, mixed economies can vary over time, in some cases, making fairly dramatic shifts in the degree and type of public involvement in a few years or decades.

Cooperative economy

As defined in this book, a cooperative economy falls within the broader definition of a mixed economy. It is a system of production, distribution, and consumption of goods and services that is primarily based on working together toward shared aims.[135] On a world scale, there can be many variations on how national and subnational economies are structured as long as the net effect is cooperative.

As I have mentioned several times, the four main, measurable components of a cooperative economy as used in the book are: increases or decreases in political democracy; increases or decreases in economic democracy; improvements in, or worsening of, quality of life; and movement toward or away from a sustainable environment. (To review basic definitions of these components, please refer to the Introduction.) Chapters 7 through 10 present more complex definitions, information on how we are doing relative to each of these measures, and how we can improve our performance in the future.

Social economies or social solidarity economies

These concepts are closely related to a cooperative economy. They refer "to a wide range of economic activities that aim to prioritize social profitability instead of purely financial profits."[136] There are a number of definitions, values, and principles associated with these concepts.[137] However, several underlying themes are shared by most of their proponents. They include the priority of meeting human needs over making a profit (mentioned above), democratic decision-making, protection of the environment, and the inadequacy of our current economic system to address these objectives.

In this book, I consider social economies and social solidarity economies to be close cousins of the cooperative economy. Since there are many variations on their use, I chose to use cooperative economy as the main theme of this book. Also, I wanted to be able to measure movement toward or away from a more cooperative economy. The four components used in this book can be used to measure whether our world economy is becoming more or less cooperative over time as well as to evaluate degrees of cooperativeness among countries and regions.

Critique of the world's current economic system

During the first 24 years of the 21st century, the world's performance on the book's main measures related to the cooperative economy has been poor to mediocre.

- Fewer than half the people on the planet have democratically elected governments. The percentage of people living in democratic countries has decreased rather than increased during the past 15 years or so.

- Economic democracy, including cooperatives, continues to be a small part of the way we do business and structure our political and social lives.

- There are vast differences in the quality of our lives, both within countries and among them. In the past few years, as measured by the United Nations, performance on several measures of quality of life have gotten worse, not better.

- We have ravaged our physical environment, especially during the past 200 years, and now face the consequences of this profligacy – especially problems related to global warming that we have brought on ourselves primarily through the burning of fossil fuels.

Each of these four measures related to an increase or decrease in the level of economic cooperation in the world are presented and analyzed in more detail in chapters 7 through 10.

Concentration of economic and political power

Why has the world economy not achieved better results on these four measures in the first quarter of the 21st century?

The underlying answer to this question is that the world economy is dominated by large corporations, an array of powerful countries with political structures that range from democratic to authoritarian, and self-serving economic and political elites. In most countries and in most international trade and other relationships, the rules and regulations (and the lack thereof) are stacked in favor of these large corporations, dominant countries, and elite individuals. This extreme maldistribution of power and wealth has resulted in a dysfunctional contemporary world economic system.

The follow-up question is: Are there strategies we can employ to make significant changes in this imbalanced world economy to make it more politically and economically democratic, to improve the quality of life, especially for people with low and moderate incomes, and to rapidly shift from dependence on fossil fuels to clean energy resources and improved energy efficiency?

As one would expect, my answer to this question is a resounding *yes*. But it's not going to be easy. The remainder of the book makes a number of recommendations related to how we can move from our current dysfunctional economy to a more cooperative and sustainable one.

Conclusion

The next chapter identifies some of the countries, organizations, and initiatives that are doing a better job than others at sowing the seeds of change that address problems related to political democracy, economic democracy, quality of life, and the sustainability of the environment. These seeds of change are the starting point for comprehensive strategies to move toward a more cooperative world economy during the next several decades.

Chapter 6

Seeds of Change

Introduction

We can't change the past, but we can learn from it and make the future a better place in which to live. The best way to accelerate positive change is to grow the seeds of transition already present in our society and economy.

The previous chapter highlighted negative economic dynamics in the first quarter of the 21st century that are inhibiting our ability to move toward a more just and environmentally sustainable world – that is, toward a more cooperative global economy. This chapter discusses the seeds of change emerging in parts of our international, national, regional, and local economies that are supportive of such a transition. These seeds of change can be nurtured to bring about a world economy that is beneficial for us as humans and for our planet.

In this chapter, the United Nations and the European Union provide examples of intergovernmental seeds of change. Then, five countries from around the globe are presented as examples of emerging cooperative economies. These national examples are followed by a discussion of businesses and other kinds of organizations and initiatives that are making (or pretending to make) serious commitments to goals other than profit-making and the concentration of wealth.

A key theme of this book reflected in this chapter is that we can make huge strides in the next couple of decades and the remainder of the 21st century toward becoming a more cooperative society in the ways we conduct our politics, social lives, and economic activities. We don't need to experience painful revolutionary up-heavals in order to make this transition. We can do it by increasing people's democratic control of their political and economic institutions, improving the quality of their lives, and addressing critically important environmental problems. The remainder of the book presents recommendations on how these changes can be made.

Inter-governmental seeds of change

Dozens of intergovernmental organizations link groups of countries around the world.[138] Examples include the World Bank, the African Union, Asia-Pacific Economic Cooperation, the Organization of American States, and many more.[139] This section of the chapter looks at the United Nations and the European Union as two of the best examples of such organizations.

United Nations

The United Nations Charter states that "The Purposes of the United Nations are:

1. To maintain international peace and security, and to that end: to take effective collective measures for the prevention and removal of threats to the peace, and for the suppression of acts of aggression or other breaches of the peace, and to bring about by peaceful means, and in conformity with the principles of justice and international law, adjustment or settlement of international disputes or situations which might lead to a breach of the peace;

2. To develop friendly relations among nations based on respect for the principle of equal rights and self-determination of peoples, and to take other appropriate measures to strengthen universal peace;

3. To achieve international co-operation in solving international problems of an economic, social, cultural, or humanitarian character, and in promoting and encouraging respect for

human rights and for fundamental freedoms for all without distinction as to race, sex, language, or religion; and

4. To be a centre for harmonizing the actions of nations in the attainment of these common ends."[140]

On the 75th anniversary of the signing of the Charter in 2020, Secretary-General António Guterres stressed its continuing importance. "At its birth, the United Nations was a symbol of global unity. Today it is the epicenter. Our mission is more important than ever."[141] The UN chief emphasized that it is only through working together that the world can fulfill ambitions such as preventing conflict, promoting sustainable development, upholding human rights, and protecting the planet. He said that "International cooperation is the only way to defeat the COVID-19 pandemic, the climate emergency, rising inequality and the spreading of hatred."[142]

Millennium Development Goals

The United Nations Millennium Declaration, signed in September 2000, committed world leaders "to combat poverty, hunger, disease, illiteracy, environmental degradation, and discrimination against women."[143] The Millennium Development Goals (MDGs) were the measurable deliverables in this Declaration. The MDG program was very successful in improving the quality of life for hundreds of millions of people around the world between 2000 and 2015.[144]

Sustainable Development Goals

The Sustainable Development Goals program is the successor UN initiative to the MDG program. It was launched in 2016 and continues to 2030. At its midpoint in 2023, the SDG program was on a trajectory to fall well short of many of its key goals, in large part due to lackluster commitment by UN member nations, the pandemic, and Russia's invasion of Ukraine.[145]

Both of these initiatives are analyzed in more detail in chapter 9.

The Paris Agreement

The Paris Agreement, also coordinated through the United Nations, went into effect in 2016 and "includes commitments from all countries to reduce their emissions and work together to adapt to the impacts of climate change…"[146] As with the SDGs in recent years, the signatories of the Paris Agreement have not been on track to achieve their goals for limiting the amount of greenhouse gas emissions going into the atmosphere, thus increasing global warming and environmental instability. Without a renewed commitment from UN members, corporations, and households around the world, we will experience continuing increases in global warming and escalating catastrophic consequences for the quality of human life and the environment. A more detailed discussion of climate change issues, including recommendations for more effective actions to address global warming and its effects, is presented in chapter 10.

Political and economic democracy

The UN's Department of Economic and Social Affairs states that it "does not advocate for a specific model of government but promotes democratic governance as a set of values and principles that should be followed for greater participation, equality, security and human development."[147]

In 1995, the UN-sponsored World Summit for Social Development – held in Copenhagen – recognized the importance of cooperatives in its people-centered approach to development and agreed to "utilize and develop fully the potential and contribution of cooperatives for the attainment of social development goals, in particular the eradication of poverty, the generation of full and productive employment, and the enhancement of social integration."[148]

Despite the problems in achieving the SDGs and climate change goals, it is important to acknowledge the critical roles the United Nations has played since its founding in 1945 in sowing seeds for a better world.

European Union

The European Union is a political and economic union formed in 1993. The EU currently consists of 27 countries with a combined population of about 450 million people (almost six percent of the world's population). This intergovernmental organization provides an example of how countries can work together to improve their collective well-being as well as to play a positive social, economic, and environmental role well beyond its members' borders.[149]

All of the 27 member countries were rated as full or flawed democracies in the Economist Intelligence Unit's (EIU's) *Democracy Index 2023*.[150] It should be noted, however, that political divisions are present within the EU, especially during the past few years. The United Kingdom withdrew from the EU at the end of 2020.[151] Hungary has received much lower democratic ratings in the past several years. Victor Orban, the prime minister of Hungary, in particular, has flaunted his white nationalist, homophobic, and pro-Russian biases in the face of the European Union's aims and values.[152]

Because of the consensus decision-making requirements in the EU, it is difficult to expel or sanction Hungary despite these violations.[153] In October 2023, Polish voters chose to move away from the authoritarian tendencies of the ruling Law and Justice Party by voting for several opposition parties. These parties have formed a moderate to progressive coalition.[154] Poland has played an active role in opposing Russia's invasion of Ukraine – in particular by providing a home, temporary respite, or transit routes for displaced Ukrainians. A recent report indicates that about 1.5 million Ukrainian refugees are now in Poland.[155]

In terms of economic and social well-being, this collection of European states stands out among the countries of the world as a positive model. There is not a single, uniform international welfare program among these countries. However, most of them share similar approaches to safeguarding the well-being of their citizens, immigrants, and visitors.

Wikipedia reports that there is a "European social model [that] generally includes an acceptance of political responsibility for levels and conditions of employment, social protections for all citizens, social inclusion, and democracy. Examples common among European countries include universal health care, free higher education, strong labor protections and regulations, and generous welfare programs in areas such as unemployment insurance, retirement pensions, and public housing."[156]

Despite energy problems resulting from EU sanctions against Russian fossil fuels after Russia's invasion of Ukraine, and Russian retaliation against these sanctions, the European Union has recently elevated its goals for reducing greenhouse gas emissions by 2050. As an article by the European Council recently summarized: "As part of the European Green Deal, with the European Climate Law, the EU has set itself a binding target of achieving climate neutrality by 2050. This requires current greenhouse gas emission levels to drop substantially in the next decades. As an intermediate step towards climate neutrality, the EU has raised its 2030 climate ambition, committing to cutting emissions by at least 55% by 2030."[157] The "Fit for 55" initiative of the European Union is analyzed in more detail in chapter 10.

The European Union is not the only organization of nations that has voluntarily formed to improve its collective well-being and that of its residents. However, despite the recent political problems with the UK and the current problems with Hungary, the EU has distinguished itself as a model from which other groups of countries around the world can learn. Recommendations for increasing the number of effective, cooperative intergovernmental organizations are presented in chapter 8.

National examples

Countries on every continent provide examples of seeds of change that may help lead to a more cooperative world economy. In particular, Denmark, Finland, Iceland, and Sweden – all members of the European Union – stand out as progressive, "seeds-of-change" countries. Norway, not part of the EU, also falls into this category.

Five "seeds-of-change" countries – one each in Africa, the Americas, Europe, Oceania, and Asia – are briefly reviewed below, with a focus on their commitments to political democracy, economic democracy, quality of life, and environmental sustainability.

Note that, with the partial exception of cooperative enterprises, there is very limited and inconsistent data on economic democracy in these countries and in most others around the world. Measurement issues related to economic democracy are addressed in greater detail in chapter 8.

Note also that these countries are by no means problem-free in these four categories, but they all provide lessons on how other countries can move in a more economically cooperative direction.

Botswana

Botswana is in southern Africa and has a population of about 2.5 million.

The country ranks in the top 20th percentile among all countries in the Economist Intelligence Unit's *Democracy Index 2023*. It has the second-highest democracy rating among all Sub-Saharan African countries.[158]

The World Bank reports that, "Living conditions have improved for the Botswana people, and poverty has fallen significantly [between 2002 and 2016]. … This rapid poverty reduction can be attributed mainly to a combination of increasing agricultural incomes, including subsidies, and demographic changes. Progress in reducing poverty has been accompanied by improvements in shared prosperity."[159]

According to Global Forest Watch, Botswana is a net sink[160] for greenhouse gases [meaning that the country absorbs more of these gases than it emits], since emissions resulting from the burning of fossil fuels are more than balanced by a net increase in the size and number of trees.[161]

On the negative side of the ledger, however, ReliefWeb, an information service of the United Nations, reports that, "Botswana is considered highly vulnerable to climate variability and change due to its high dependence on rain-fed agriculture and natural resources, high levels of poverty – particularly in rural areas – and a low adaptive capacity to deal with these expected changes. Primary challenges are centered around water resource availability, changing precipitation patterns, and increasing population demands. Climatic and socio-economic environments in semi-arid areas in Botswana make communities vulnerable to food insecurity and unstable livelihoods as well as unsustainable agroecological systems, crop failure, and unproductive rangelands."[162]

Overall, however, Botswana scores well on the measures related to a cooperative economy, and provides a positive example to other countries, especially in Africa.

Costa Rica

Costa Rica is a heavily forested country in Central America with a population of about five million. It spans from the Pacific Ocean to the Atlantic Ocean.

Costa Rica ranks 17th among the countries in the *Democracy Index 2023* and is one of the highest-rated democracies among developing countries.[163]

According to OECD (the Organization for Economic Cooperation and Development), "Costa Rica has made considerable progress in improving the quality of life of its citizens over the past decade. Notwithstanding these improvements, the OECD's *Better Life Index* rates Costa Rica as underperforming in income, jobs, education, social connections, civic engagement, safety and life satisfaction."[164]

Based on a study by the Rand Corporation, "[I]n the race to cut carbon emissions, Costa Rica has been leading the way. It adopted its own plan in 2019, promising to show the world what a net-zero carbon future could look like. Its plan would transform almost every facet of its economy, from car sales to cattle farming."[165]

Iceland

Iceland is an island country between Greenland and Northern Europe with a population of under 400,000.

Iceland scores third out of all of the countries measured on the *Democracy Index 2023.*[166]

According to the Organization for Economic Cooperation and Development (OECD), "Iceland performs well in many dimensions of well-being relative to other countries in the *Better Life Index*. Iceland outperforms the average in jobs, health, environmental quality, social connections, civic engagement, safety and life satisfaction. It underperforms the average in education."[167]

"Iceland aims to achieve carbon neutrality before 2040 and to cut greenhouse gas emissions by 40% by 2030 under the Paris Agreement.... Iceland's emissions profile is unusual in many ways. Almost all heating and electricity generation is provided by renewables – in particular, hydro and geothermal energy. Iceland has great potential for carbon uptake from the atmosphere by afforestation and revegetation, and to curb emissions from soils by reclaiming drained wetlands. The biggest sources of emissions (outside land use) are industrial processes, road transport, agriculture, fisheries and waste management."[168]

Kiribati

Kiribati is a small country in the central Pacific Ocean composed of 33 islands, with a population of about 120,000.[169]

The country is not included in the *Democracy Index 2023*, but was ranked in the top 20% in the world in the *Freedom in the World 2024* published by Freedom House.[170]

On the negative side, Kiribati has a low standard of living with a very small gross domestic product and is considered to be one of the least developed countries in the world.[171]

About a decade ago, there was concern in the island group that Kiribati would become the first country in the world to disappear under the sea as a result of global warming. The government purchased a tract of land on a nearby Fijian island so that it could relocate its population when the country's islands were no longer habitable. More recent scientific evidence, however, indicates that the island chain is not in any immediate danger of disappearing. The land purchased in Fiji is now being developed for agriculture and is no longer seen as a refuge from climate disaster.[172]

Because of its small size and population, and its low level of development, Kiribati's net carbon emissions are negligible. The country's climate change priority policy goals focus on coastal protection and infrastructure, food security, water security, energy security (including a major shift to renewable energy), environmental sustainability and resilience, and health security.[173]

South Korea

South Korea's democracy is ranked 22nd of all the countries in the world in the *Democracy Index 2023*.[174]

According to OECD, "Korea performs well across a number of well-being dimensions relative to other countries in the *Better Life Index*. Korea outperforms the average in education, health and civic engagement. It underperforms the average in environmental quality, social connections and life satisfaction."[175]

An Associated Press article reported in October 2021 that, "South Korea set a new goal for fighting climate change over the next decade, saying it will aim to cut its greenhouse gas emissions to 40% below 2018 levels by 2030. … South Korea aims to be carbon neutral by 2050."[176]

Summary of country-level examples

The five countries reviewed above provide examples of seeds of change that are improving the lives of people and the sustainability of the planet. They also rank well in their levels of democracy. They provide a mix of developed and developing countries, but in each case are taking actions to maintain and improve the quality of life of their citizens. In terms of climate change policies and practices, each of these countries is implementing strategies that fit its unique circumstances. As a group, they are preforming well above the international average in reducing and/or adapting to problems related to global warming.

Chapters 7 through 10 present recommendations for other countries to learn from these examples, and to develop their own strategies for becoming more politically and economically democratic, improving the lives of their citizens, and expanding efforts to reduce global warming.

Businesses and other non-governmental organizations

Most of us tend to think of the non-governmental part of the economy in terms of the financial performance of for-profit businesses. This section of the chapter makes the case that the private sector of the economy is far more complex and diversified than that. In fact, many of the seeds of change leading toward a more cooperative world economy are flourishing in those parts of the private economy that are not primarily profit-driven, many of which are locally or community focused.

Cooperatively owned businesses

Cooperatives (or co-ops) are a unique business form because they are owned and democratically controlled by the people and organizations to which they provide services. That is, their very structure is based on economic democracy. Their primary goal is serving their members rather than making a profit. (Of course, they need to be profitable in the long term in order to stay in business, but that is not their primary *raison d'être*.)

Each year, the International Cooperative Alliance[177] and Euricse (the European Union Research Institute on Cooperatives and Social Enterprises)[178] jointly publish a *World Cooperative Monitor* report which provides data on the largest 300 cooperatives in the world.[179] Although a valuable research resource on cooperatives, it does not provide much information on the overall number and variety of cooperatives around the world.

The Global Census on Cooperatives, published in 2014,[180] quantified the impact of cooperatives in almost every country in the world. However, because it was a one-time event, the census does not provide the basis for longitudinal analysis of cooperative performance.

Thus, there is a large research gap in the measurement of worldwide cooperative performance over time. A major recommendation of this book is that a global cooperative census be conducted every five years so that we can determine whether there is an increase or a decrease in the impact of cooperatives overall, in specific cooperative sectors, by country and in the world. Without such measurement, we are only "guestimating" what the long-term influence of co-ops in society is, and what actions to take to improve co-op performance over time.

I discuss in more detail the measurement shortcomings related to cooperatives and other aspects of economic democracy in chapter 8. In the meantime, following is a brief introduction to the cooperative business model.

According to its website, the International Cooperative Alliance unites, represents, and serves cooperatives worldwide.

"Founded in 1895, it is one of the oldest non-governmental organisations and one of the largest ones measured by the number of people represented: 1 billion cooperative members on the planet.

"It is the apex body representing cooperatives, which are estimated to be around 3 million worldwide, providing a global voice and forum for knowledge, expertise and co-ordinated action for and about cooperatives."[181]

Even with these impressive numbers, cooperatives account for only a small percentage of the world gross product (that is, the sum of all the national gross products in the world). Thus, co-ops are pervasive but not a large part of the world's economy. However, because they operate in virtually every business sector and country in the world, they have tremendous potential to have a major impact on expanding the world's cooperative economy.

As a result of this potential, most of chapter 8 is devoted to a strategic analysis of ways in which cooperatives can play a much more expanded role in the next few decades in facilitating the emergence of a more cooperative world economy.

Other examples of economic democracy

Co-ops are not the only component of economic democracy. Many businesses that are not formal cooperatives operate under cooperative principles. These include some microfinance organizations and other self-help groups. Other examples of economic democracy include labor unions and other labor advocacy organizations, and consumer- and community-advocacy organizations. Additional examples and a more detailed analysis of economic democracy are presented in chapter 8.

Socially and environmentally responsible for-profit businesses

During the past two decades or so, an increasing number of for-profit businesses and business-rating services have begun to emphasize the social, environmental, and governance goals and accomplishments of their enterprises. The often-used phrase for these activities is "environmental, social and corporate governance" (ESG, for short).[182]

According to Wikipedia, "In less than 20 years, the ESG movement has grown from a corporate social responsibility initiative launched by the United Nations into a global phenomenon representing more than US$30 trillion in assets under management."[183]

Some of these corporations and rating systems should be lauded for their roles in carrying out and calling attention to ESG initiatives. However, there are serious problems with the way many corporations and investment funds abuse the concepts of social, environmental, and other aspects of corporate responsibility.

Following is an excerpt from an *Investopia* article on this topic. "Greenwashing is the process of conveying a false impression or providing misleading information about how a company's products are more environmentally sound. Greenwashing is considered an unsubstantiated claim to deceive consumers into believing that a company's products are environmentally friendly.

"For example, companies involved in greenwashing behavior might make claims that their products are from recycled materials or have energy-saving benefits. Although some of the environmental claims might be partly true, companies engaged in greenwashing typically exaggerate their claims or the benefits in an attempt to mislead consumers."[184]

This kind of propaganda on environmental behavior is particularly egregious in the fossil fuels sector. Similar misleading claims are applied by some companies to their social and governance activities.[185]

Another distorting factor is the overstatement of the ESG performance of for-profit companies in order to encourage investors to buy specific stocks and exchange-traded funds (ETFs).

Notwithstanding, the self-aggrandizing corporate abuses of greenwashing and other misrepresentations of ESG performance, companies that clearly define and evaluate measures of economic, social, and environmental responsibility – and then take actions to improve their performance – are contributing to a more cooperative economy.

Not-for-profit organizations

There are many not-for-profit organizations that serve the needs of people around the world. Cornell University's Legal Information Institute defines this kind of organization in part as, "[A] group organized for purposes other than generating profit and in which no part of the organization's income is distributed to its members, directors, or officers. Non-profit corporations are often termed 'non-stock corporations.' They can take the form of a corporation, an individual enterprise (for example, individual charitable contributions), unincorporated association, partnership, [or a] foundation..."[186]

The Foundation Group recently calculated that there are more than 10 million nonprofit organizations around the world.[187] According to the Urban Institute, the nonprofit sector contributed approximately $1 trillion to the US national economy in 2016 or about 5.6% of the gross domestic product.[188]

Just as with corporations that pretend to espouse ESG goals, not all nonprofits and foundations come anywhere near meeting a "public good criterion for their donations and activities."[189]

In 2022, the *New York Times* reported on an extreme example of a politically motivated abuse of nonprofit organizational status that has nothing to do with the advancement of the public good. "A new conservative nonprofit group scored a $1.6 billion windfall last year via a little-known donor — an extraordinary sum that could give Republicans and their causes a huge financial boost ahead of the midterms, and for years to come. The source of the money was Barre Seid, an electronics manufacturing mogul, and the donation is among the largest – if not the largest – single contribution ever made to a politically focused nonprofit."[190]

Individuals, groups, and local communities

Greta Thunberg

In August 2018, Greta Thunberg, at the time, a 15-year-old Swedish high school student – along with a few friends – organized a one-day school strike on the climate change crisis. Shortly after, the Friday strikes became a weekly event called "Fridays for Future." The Friday strikes soon became an international event involving hundreds of thousands of teenagers, as well as others supportive of climate change reform.[191]

Thunberg addressed a UN Summit on climate change in September 2019 with a speech that included the following words, "I shouldn't be up here. I should be back in school on the other side of the ocean, yet you all come to us young people for hope. How dare you?"[192] In 2021, she said politicians' promises have been 30 years of "blah blah blah."[193]

So, yes. Individuals can make a difference in calling attention to social, economic, and environmental problems, and in helping to find solutions to them.

But, individuals can't do it alone. They need other people with whom to work to accomplish their shared goals. Following is an example of an "adoption-of-change" activity that can be carried out by individuals, groups, and local communities.

Cleaning up Madison's lakes

This example is a personal story. I live in Madison, Wisconsin, in the United States. I love this city for a lot of reasons, including the presence of the University of Wisconsin where I got my graduate degree in sociology, the city's Goldilocks size of about 250,000 people, and the myriad bike, running, and walking paths that allow us to go just about anywhere in or near the city safely and energy efficiently.

What I like the most about the Madison area are the lakes among which the city is located. However, these lakes are threatened as a result of increasing phosphorus pollution during the past 75 years or so. The primary source of the phosphorus? Farms in the upper part of the watershed that produce runoff from land saturated with cow manure and chemical fertilizers containing phosphorus.

The results? Murky water where residents used to be able to see all the way to the bottom, even in deep water; a proliferation of aquatic weeds; green algae blooms that stink and make swimming undesirable; and blue-green algae blooms that are toxic to humans and pets. So, what should be the most attractive resource in our community has become, to exaggerate a bit, more and more like a collection of large cesspools.

Fortunately, that's not the end of the story. People in the community have been concerned about the deterioration of the lakes for a long time, but we didn't do much about it. A little over a decade ago, the county, the city, and a new nonprofit organization – the Clean Lakes Alliance – began making a concerted effort to reduce the phosphorus runoff into the lakes.

Those efforts are bearing fruit. Less phosphorus is flowing into the lakes as a result of improved farming practices, buffers along the lakes' edges, manure digesters that remove phosphorus and create a biogas substitute for "natural" gas, and other measures.

Probably the most important remediation technique is just around the corner – a manure processing facility to be located in the area of the watershed that has the biggest concentration of cows. This new facility will very probably be a key factor in changing the watershed from a net importer of phosphorus for the past 75 years to a net exporter. We should see visibly cleaner, clearer, and more swimmable lakes in the decades ahead.

Thousands of thumbs have gone into trying to plug the phosphorus-leaking dykes in our watershed. The process became effective when the county, city, staff and members of the Clean Lakes Alliance, farm leaders, and many area residents made the lake clean-up a priority issue.

I can claim a modest role in this process, having served on a number of committees since the early 2000s, and pushing the "phosphate-balance" theme – that is, increasing exports and decreasing imports of this harmful chemical. I even convinced a county committee to insert language in a recent resolution on this issue, which included the importance of periodically measuring changes in the P-balance of the lakes.

"Think globally and act locally" is not just a catchphrase. It's the means by which each of us can be agents of positive change – whether we're voting for candidates and referenda that benefit the community; installing solar panels on our roofs or in our neighborhoods; walking, biking, taking public transport or driving electric cars; volunteering at the local food bank or in a senior housing center; shopping at farmers' markets and locally owned, community-oriented businesses; donating to causes, such as aid to Ukraine and others that we feel strongly about, and more.

The preface to the book emphasized that individuals can be subjects of history, not just its objects. This section of chapter 6 reinforces that message.

Conclusion

This chapter has identified some inter-governmental organizations, countries, and other organizations and initiatives that provide examples of seeds of change that are nurturing political and economic democracy, quality of life, and the sustainability of the environment leading toward a more cooperative world economy.

The chapter also identified organizations and individuals that are sowing weeds rather than productive seeds of change, for example, greenwashing and abuses of nonprofit status. The remaining chapters of the book recommend strategies for building on the positive seeds of change to bring about an emerging cooperative world economy during the next several decades of the 21st century.

Chapter 7

Political Democracy: A Precondition for a Cooperative Economy

Introduction

The role of democracy in a cooperative economy

As I wrote in the introduction to the book, a cooperative economy puts the well-being of the many ahead of the wealth and power of a few. The best form of government to achieve this outcome is political democracy.

Theoretically, "the well-being of the many" can be achieved in a country ruled by a benevolent dictator or oligarchy. But that's a rare occurrence, and one that is prone to deteriorate into self-serving leadership for the simple reason that there are no checks and balances that maintain the benevolent disposition of the rulers from year to year and generation to generation.

Bhutan

Bhutan, a small country located between China and India, provides an example that is an exception to this pattern. The country was ruled for almost a century by the same royal family. In 2001, however, the king announced that Bhutan would transition from an absolute monarchy to a constitutional monarchy (a la the United Kingdom). As a result, a constitution was passed in 2005, and the first democratic elections for parliament occurred in 2007.[194] Overall, the transition is going very well, although the Democracy Index 2023 rates the country as a "hybrid regime," meaning that it has not fully transitioned to a democratic country.[195]

Bhutan represents an unusual example in which the ruler himself initiated the transition to a democratic government. In the vast majority of cases, absolute monarchs and other authoritarian rulers don't willingly give up power. They are forced to abdicate by popular unrest, a coup, or a takeover by a more powerful country.

Key components of political democracy

One of the hallmarks of democracy is that power is required to be periodically re-affirmed or change hands through "free and fair elections." No individual, family, or group rules indefinitely. Since a cooperative economy is based on the premise that "the well-being of the many" is maintained over long periods of time, it is important that there are institutionalized means (e.g., a constitution, and separation of powers among the executive, legislative, and judicial branches of government) to maintain this commitment through popular elections. Thus, democratic governments play a critical role in creating and maintaining cooperative economies.

Classification of different kinds of governments

In the analysis of democracy used in this book, I rely heavily on the definition and measurement of democracy developed by the Economist Intelligence Unit (EIU). The EIU's "democracy index is based on the ratings for 60 indicators, grouped into five categories: electoral process and pluralism; civil liberties; the functioning of government; political participation; and political culture." The countries and regions of the world are divided into four types of government using the above indicators: full democracies, flawed democracies, hybrid regimes, and authoritarian regimes. The EIU has published an annual democracy index report since 2006.[196]

Organization of the chapter

The chapter is divided into two main sections: historical trends in democracy and strategies for increasing democracy in the future.

Historical trends in democracy

Chimps, early humans, and democratic experiments during the past few millennia

Some primatologists and anthropologists maintain that groups of our primate relatives and of human hunter-gatherers practiced various forms of consensus decision-making.[197] Examples include collectively organizing activities related to meeting the basic necessities of life, deciding to migrate (or stay put), and protecting themselves from enemies, including other groups of primates or humans.[198]

A great deal of literature about democracy can be found dating back as far as 3,000 years ago in ancient Phoenicia, Greece, Rome, and various city-states, empires, and tribal groups on every inhabited continent. One form of early democracy was assemblies of eligible male citizens in which a variety of governance-related decisions were made. In general, lower-class males, women, and slaves were excluded from these gatherings.[199]

Although lessons can be learned from these early forms of democracy, these lessons will not be the focus of this chapter. Instead, I concentrate on the history of political democracies during the past 250 years or so.

The United States: the first modern, but flawed, democracy

Many historians cite the United States as developing the first modern democracy. The American Declaration of Independence, written in 1776, asserts that "All men are created equal, that they are endowed by their Creator with certain unalienable Rights, that among these are Life, Liberty and the pursuit of Happiness."[200]

This declaration was followed in 1788 by the adoption of the U.S. Constitution, which "provides the world's first formal blueprint for a modern democracy."[201] Some of the framers of the Constitution and later historians contend that key elements of the Constitution were derived from the structure of the Iroquois Federation, a grouping of six Native American tribes in eastern North America that began in the early years of European colonization and lasted for about 200 years.[202] The Iroquois provided a model for the 13 British colonies to establish a "united" country that retained some of the unique characteristics of each former colony.

What led up to this Declaration and Constitution was an increasingly bitter rift between Great Britain and its colonies in eastern North America. These colonies were well situated to break away from their mother country and make the transition to a new, independent nation. They were adjacent to one another and were ruled by the same king. The initial immigrants who settled in these colonies were primarily of British descent. Some of them were highly educated. These settlements were not like many colonies in which indigenous populations were relatively easy to subjugate because of huge technological gaps, especially armaments, and political divisions among themselves. In the American colonies, the indigenous inhabitants had been depopulated through diseases imported by the colonists, subjugated, and/or forced to relocate out of the colonies.

In the 1760s and '70s, Britain exploited and sought to dominate the colonies through "taxation without representation,"[203] the garrisoning of troops in American cities, and other heavy-handed measures. However, it was difficult for Britain to enforce these punitive actions and maintain a military presence in the colonies because of the monetary cost of governance and the distance between Britain and North America.

All of these factors provided the colonists with a unique opportunity to revolt against the British crown. One could even argue that the colonies as a group were a kind of cooperative because of their common cause against the British, and the fact that they needed each other in order to break away from British rule.

Historians differ on how disgruntlement over taxes and other overbearing actions by the British turned into a war of independence. The perspective that is most convincing to me is that the British escalation of the tax laws into the heightened presence of troops in the colonies and the violent actions against colonists that ensued changed many of the colonists from protesters to revolutionaries.

Until British soldiers resorted to violence, the colonists were content with griping and protesting about taxes and other indignities as British subjects. But suppression caused many colonists to change their quest for justice within the British Empire to seeking independence from it.

Although one can cite the heroic actions of many colonists in their fight for independence and democracy, it is important to recognize the many flaws in this new "democracy."

Voting restrictions

Each of the 13 colonies became a state after the war of independence. Except where specified in the Constitution, voting requirements were set at the state level. During the early years of the country, voting was highly restricted.

As cited in Wikipedia, "Generally, states limited [the right to vote] to property-owning or tax-paying white males (about 6% of the population). However, some states allowed.... Black males to vote, and New Jersey also included unmarried and widowed women, regardless of color. Since married women were not allowed to own property, they could not meet the property qualifications."[204]

Even today, state-based rules for voting, such as the number and location of voting places and gerrymandering (the geographical shaping of voting districts within a state, usually to favor white voters or a specific political party), have resulted in uneven voting rights from state to state.[205]

States' rights

The founding fathers built a number of states' rights into the Constitution and other federal laws for the simple reason that they needed to establish a consensus among 13 former colonies with different-sized populations and varying economies and political orientations.

Some states' rights can be justified based on the intent of having decentralized political decision-making within the country that takes into account the specific circumstances of each state. However, one negative consequence of states' rights is the granting of more power at the national level to small states than to large ones.

Two examples of this power imbalance are that each state elects two U.S. senators, and that the president and vice-president are elected by the Electoral College rather than by popular vote. California is currently the most populous state, with about 40 million inhabitants. Wyoming is the smallest, with fewer than 600,000 people.[206] Despite their vast differences in population, each state elects two U.S. senators. The Electoral College, which has a built-in bias toward smaller states, has elected the president and vice-president who lost the popular vote four times in American history – 1876, 1888, 2000, and 2016.[207]

Persecution and discrimination

The decimation of indigenous people in the Americas began with the arrival of Columbus and his cohorts in 1492 and continued with the earliest European settlements in the Americas.[208] One source estimates that almost 60 million indigenous people, amounting to about 90% of their total population, died in the first hundred years of European settlement in the Americas from European and African diseases, warfare, and massacres.[209]

Portuguese traders brought the first African slaves to Jamestown not long after it was originally settled.[210] A slave economy dominated the southern states until Abraham Lincoln's Emancipation Proclamation, delivered on January 1, 1863, in which he stated that all slaves in the "rebellious" states "henceforward shall be free."[211] Almost three years later, New Jersey was the last state in the country to formally abolish slavery.[212]

After Lincoln's assassination in 1865, "Reconstruction" (bringing the southern states back into the Union and guaranteeing rights to former slaves)[213] lasted a little over a decade, when the federal government abdicated its role of protecting and advancing the emancipation of slaves, leading to the second-class status of Blacks in America.[214]

Immigrants, especially Asians, often had to serve a period of indentured servitude, "in which [they] contracted to work without salary for a specific number of years." Many indentured servants lived in squalid conditions and had no voting rights and very limited other legal rights.[215]

Corruption

"Corruption in the United States has been a perennial political issue, peaking in the Jacksonian era [in the second quarter of the 19th century] and the Gilded Age [in the fourth quarter of the 19th century] before declining with the reforms of the Progressive Era [primarily in the first quarter of the 20th century]. As of 2022, the United States is the 27th least-corrupt country in the world according to the *Corruption Perceptions Index 2023*."[216]

Most recently, Donald Trump's presidency, which lasted from January 2017 to January 2021, brought a new wave of corruption to the United States. During his time in office, Trump was impeached twice by the House of Representatives. In the aftermath of his presidency, Trump, the Trump organization, and some of his acolytes and supporters faced civil and criminal indictments, some of which will probably continue to be prosecuted well after this book is published.[217]

American foreign policy

"The United States has been involved in numerous foreign interventions throughout its history. By the broadest definition of military intervention, the U.S. has engaged in nearly 400 military interventions between 1776 and 2019, with half of these operations occurring since 1950 and over 25% occurring in the post-Cold War period."[218] One study concluded that the U.S. was involved in at least 81 interventions in foreign elections between 1946 and 2000.[219]

"From the late 1950s, the CIA was involved more or less directly in plots to assassinate several foreign leaders. Among them was Cuba's Fidel Castro, Congo's Patrice Lumumba, and the Dominican Republic's Rafael Trujillo. In the mid-1970s, a series of revelations about the CIA's involvement in assassination attempts prompted numerous inquiries by the government and Congress."[220]

This interventionist history doesn't exactly validate the role of the United States as a beacon of democracy in the world.

The positive side of U.S. democracy

Despite the many flaws in American democracy since the birth of the country, it has continued to preserve its basic tenets and has served as a model for other countries (although in the aftermath of the 2020 election, Donald Trump and his supporters have been undermining this democratic model).[221]

A key example of these core tenets is the basic structure of the Constitution, which simultaneously provides for political stability and gradual reform. Twenty-seven amendments have been made to the Constitution since it was first ratified.[222]

A second key feature of the Constitution is the balancing of power that it created among the executive branch, the legislature, and the judiciary, which greatly reduces the likelihood of a usurpation of power by any one group.

The expansion of modern democracies

Not only did democracy in the United States evolve in the 19th and 20th centuries, but new democracies sprang up in other parts of the world as well. According to the World Economic Forum, ten countries became democratic by about 1900. In order of the age of their democracies, these countries are the United States, Switzerland, New Zealand, Canada, the United Kingdom, Luxembourg, Belgium, the Netherlands, Norway, and Australia.[223] Note that all of the above are either Western European countries or former British colonies.

We can look at the spread of democracy in the world somewhat systematically, thanks in large part to Polity Project IV, which charted the development of democracies between 1800 and the early 2100s.[224] Note that these data refer to the number of democratic countries, not to the number of people living in democracies. For example, two of the largest countries in the world in the late 1900s were China and Russia, both authoritarian countries.

The Polity Project data show that there were just a couple of democracies in the world until the mid-1800s, then a gradual increase to about 20 by the early 1930s. A steep drop back to about 10 occurred in the early 1940s. There was a rapid rise in the number of democracies to the high 30s from the mid-1940s to the late 1980s, and an even steeper increase to about 80 democracies by the end of the 20th century.[225]

This pattern of democratic progress can be mostly explained by five changes in the world's political landscape during the 1800s and 1900s:

1. The shift to democracies in European and former British colonies during the 1800s (cited above)

2. A number of Latin American colonies gaining independence in the late 1800s and early 1900s

3. Limited decolonization after World War I

4. The post-World War II decolonization of many parts of Africa and Asia

5. The break-up of the Soviet Union and Yugoslavia from 1989 to 1991

At the end of the 20th century, the Polity IV Project reported that, in addition to the estimated 80 democracies in the world, there were 50 "anocracies" (regimes that mix democratic with autocratic features) and 60 autocracies (or authoritarian regimes).[226]

In summary, dramatic growth in the number of democracies took place between the late 1700s and 2000, by which time they constituted the largest political category of the world's countries.

Backsliding in the first quarter of the 21st century

According to the reports of the Economist Intelligence Unit's Democracy Index[227] and Freedom House's Freedom in the World Index,[228] democracy has declined during the first quarter of the 21st century.

These two indices use slightly different methodologies to measure changes in democracy from year to year. In the Democracy Index reports, "countries are rated as full democracies, flawed democracies, hybrid regimes, or authoritarian regimes."[229] Freedom House classifies countries as free, partly free, or not free based on measures of the degree of civil liberties and political rights.[230] Despite their different methodologies, the two indices correlate very highly in their country ratings.

As I wrote in my March 2022 newsletter, "For the past 16 years, the EIU's Democracy Index has been on a downward trend. The

Freedom House Index has shown a similar negative pattern for 17 years. That is, the countries of the world have become less democratic and more authoritarian during most of the 21st century to date."[231]

There appears to be a number of factors that explain this recent weakening of democracy. Many of the new democracies established from the 1960s to the early 1990s were fragile to begin with. In general, they had weak or no constitutions, one dominant political party, high levels of corruption, power-hungry leaders who aspired to be presidents or prime ministers for life rather than for terms set by law, and/or citizens who were not mobilized to counter these autocratic tendencies.

Thus, autocracies or dysfunctional, quasi-democracies developed in many African, Asian, and Latin American countries in post-colonial times, as well as in a few European countries that had been part of the Soviet Union or that had emerged after the break-up of Yugoslavia.

Although independence had been achieved in the 1800s by many Latin American countries, these same anti-democratic phenomena occurred in a number of them as well, complicated in the latter part of the 20th century and the first quarter of the 21st century by powerful and violent drug cartels in certain countries, which bought the services of many officials at all levels of government with generous bribes, threatened them and their families, and assassinated some of them.

International polling conducted by the Pew Foundation reveals a broad preference for democratic governance over authoritarian governance among the people surveyed.[232] The problem appears to be translating these democratic aspirations into lasting changes in political institutions.

Arab Spring

For example, the "Arab Spring" protests, which began in late 2010 with the self-immolation of a street vendor in Tunisia, spread to approximately 18 countries in North Africa and the Middle East during the next two years.[233] *However, few lasting changes in the autocratic governments of these countries resulted from these protests.*

As Time *magazine reported in January 2021, "What this shows is that the drivers of uprisings are different [from] those of democratic transition. The former are driven by the persistent socio-economic and political dysfunctions widespread in the Arab world; democratic transitions, meanwhile, require particular enabling conditions. These include a national pro-democracy movement that can not only organize mass protests but also win elections; a set of state institutions, at least some of which (the army in most cases) would enable such a transition; and a regional environment that is supportive, or at least accommodating. So far, this has rarely been the case."*[234]

The struggle for democracy may be approaching a turning point

The downward trend in democracy may be about to turn upward. However, the most recent annual reports of both the Democracy Index and the Freedom in the World Index indicate that the number of countries with democratic ratings was still declining relative to authoritarian ones in 2023.[235] [236]

Moscow's war of aggression appears to have galvanized democracies in Europe, the United States, Canada, and other countries to come to Ukraine's aid by providing both military and humanitarian assistance.

As stated in the EIU's *Democracy Index 2023*, "By far the biggest event of [2022] was Russia's full-scale invasion of Ukraine…, a flagrant violation of Ukrainian sovereignty that sent shockwaves around the world. Russia's actions have brought home to many the vital importance of defending national sovereignty, without which real freedom and democracy are unattainable."[237]

There have been three major consequences not intended by Putin's "special military operation": strong, effective resistance by the Ukrainian government and its people to the invasion; an outpouring of support for Ukraine by European and other democratic countries; and a level of political, economic, and military cooperation among these democracies that has not been seen since the end of World War II.

This rallying around the flag of Ukraine's democracy is reminiscent of what happened during and after World War II. Western democracies united to defeat the Axis powers. After the war, there was a flowering of democracy around the world.

However, according to *Democracy Index 2022*, "[M]any countries in the Global South have not followed the US, UK, the EU and others in taking sides against Russia. Their reluctance to line up behind Western countries reflects, variously, the advantage of taking a neutral position because not taking sides serves their own short-term self-interest; frustration with the established international order; resentment of perceived Western hypocrisy in the context of past Western meddling and intervention in their affairs; and dependency on Russian minerals and other resources. The principle of national sovereignty is too important to be sacrificed on the altar of anti-Westernism, but the inconsistent application of the principle by Western powers has bred cynicism that is now making it more difficult for Western countries to attract support from the Global South."[238]

How can we increase the number of people living in democratic countries in the second quarter of the century?
The *Democracy Index* estimates that 45% of the world's population (about 3.6 billion people) lives in full or flawed democracies.[239]

So, how do we get from 45% to over 50%? The answer to this question is a complex one, and, in any case, no one can predict the future. However, following are a few recommendations that address this question and the related one of how we can move toward a cooperative world economy by mid-century.

Despite the decline in democracies in the first quarter of the 21st century, major opportunities exist to turn the tide in the second quarter. Following are five key recommendations that can help make this happen:

1. Learn from history the lessons about democracy and autocracy in the 19th and 20th centuries.

2. Increase country-level, domestic popular pressure for change that is combined with the development of effective political institutions to implement and sustain democracy.

3. Build international cooperation on combating global warming and ameliorating its negative effects on humans and the planet.

4. Apply international incentives and sanctions to countries that are impeding efforts to increase, or not doing their fair share in increasing, democracy around the world.

5. Focus economic incentives (and sanctions, if necessary) on expanding democracy and human rights in the world's largest countries – India, China, the United States, Indonesia, Pakistan, Nigeria, and Brazil.[240]

1

Learn from history

First of all, we can learn from the history of democracies and autocracies during the past two centuries in order to strengthen democracies in the future. Major historical lessons include the following:

- Enacting, and adhering to, democratic constitutions. This is a lesson from the formation of the United States, European Union member countries, and other modern democracies. Countries with "full democracies" and international organizations, especially the United Nations, can help less democratic and non-democratic countries become more democratic, especially through economic development assistance that incentivizes and rewards democratic behavior in recipient countries.

- Establishing and maintaining a balance of power among different branches of government. An executive, legislative, and judicial balance of power can avoid an overly powerful executive branch, which is one of the biggest threats to democracy. The same kinds of targeted international aid mentioned in the above paragraph applies to the checks and balances proposed here.

2

Increase country-level, domestic popular pressure for change

- *Support, rather than undermine, other countries' democracies.* This is a lesson from the United States, European colonizers (including the Soviet Union and Germany), and China. In this case, the recommendation is to provide genuinely constructive development assistance and to avoid the economic exploitation of developing countries that too often prevents them from becoming truly independent nations.

- *Recognize that protests alone aren't enough to build democracies.* As the Arab Spring protests clearly show, it's not enough to express mass opposition to autocratic regimes. Protests need to be accompanied by "lasting changes in political institutions."[241] The ingredients for a successful transition to democracy include:
  - Popular support for change, including well-organized, preferably non-violent, protests
  - Two or more strong political parties
  - Free and fair elections
  - Freedom of the press/communications

- A carefully crafted constitution that is adhered to by political leaders
- Effective governmental institutions that include enforceable "checks and balances" among the executive, the legislative, and the judiciary branches of government
- An international community that helps to develop and sustain countries' democracies

3

Combating and adapting to global warming

Many people around the world, including me, agree with the scientific consensus that human-made global warming is the biggest threat to plant and animal (including human) life on the planet. Therefore, combating climate change has the potential to galvanize the most important cooperative activity of our lifetimes. As a result, we need to take the following actions:

- *Create and maintain a genuine, worldwide commitment to climate change reform.* Global temperature increases negatively affect every country in the world. Thus, reducing greenhouse gas emissions and ameliorating the impacts of a warming climate are in all of our long-term interests. There are way too many "pretend" and half-hearted pronouncements and public relations gimmicks by countries, corporations, politicians, and conspiracy theorists related to climate action, but not enough constructive action. A united approach to decreasing carbon emissions can lead to united actions in other spheres as well, including supporting the stability and growth of democratic countries.

  - Governments and corporations should recognize the indisputable fact that action on climate change will be far less expensive now than it will be later and, in fact, can be a significant part of improving economic and employment conditions in both developing and developed countries.
  - The UN's bureaucratically phrased and unenforceable "nationally determined contributions" – the goals set by each country under the Paris Agreement that are intended to

address climate change problems – must be dramatically strengthened and adhered to in order to have a significant impact on reducing global warming by 2050.

- Developed countries need to increase their technical and financial assistance to developing countries in order to accelerate the world's transition away from fossil fuels and to help protect developing countries from some of the negative, climate-related consequences of global warming.

- Local communities and individuals can and should become much more knowledgeable about the negative consequences of global warming and play an active role in changing their climate-related behavior.

4

Sanctions and incentives

Both sanctions and incentives should be used to increase democracy. "Carrots and sticks" can be effective means to get countries and corporations to increase their commitment to democratic forms of government. How might this work? Countries that are serious about increasing democracy can take economic actions that encourage greater commitment to this goal by laggard countries, corporations, communities, and individuals.

- Carrots are generally more effective than sticks in changing behavior, so financial incentives should be the priority. One example already underway is an agreement between several developed countries and South Africa to clean up the latter's fossil fuel-dependent economy.[242] This is part of a United Nations initiative to assist developing countries in achieving both democracy-building and climate change goals.[243]

- Inevitably, there will be countries and corporations that won't respond to these financial incentives and will continue to undermine democracy. This is where the sticks come into play. The United States, Canada, European Union members, and other countries are currently sanctioning Russia – including taking steps to reduce Russian international revenue from oil and gas sales – because of its invasion of Ukraine. The same kind of sanctions could be applied to other countries that undermine democracy at home and abroad. Sanctions should include tariffs and other financial instruments that deter anti-democratic actions.

- The international response to the Russian invasion of Ukraine discussed briefly above presents a good example of both sanctions and incentives – sanctions against Russia, especially in the form of negative economic and political actions, and incentives for Ukraine, including military and humanitarian aid. A third result of these concerted steps by democratic countries is to present an example of democracy-building (and democracy-preserving) actions that groups of countries can take.

5

Focus democratic reform efforts on the world's largest countries

To achieve the goal of having most of the people in the world living in democracies by 2050, it is critical to support democratic reforms in the world's largest countries.

For example, India recently surpassed China as the most populous country in the world. Demographers predict that the population growth rate in India will continue to outpace that of China for decades to come.

India is rated as a "flawed democracy" in Democracy Index 2023.[244] *Since becoming prime minister in 2014, Narendra Modi, supported by a Hindu nationalist political party, has increasingly violated the civil rights of some of India's citizens, especially Muslims, and has limited freedom of the press.*[245]

Because of its large population, India alone would significantly reduce the number of people in the world living in democracies if its drift toward authoritarianism should continue in the coming years. Therefore, it is critical that Indian voters and well-established democratic countries convince Modi and whoever should succeed him as prime minister to stay in the democratic fold.

- Other large countries include China, the United States, Indonesia, Brazil, Pakistan, and Nigeria. All have populations above 200 million. The United States, Indonesia, and Brazil are classified as flawed democracies by the *Democracy Index 2023.*[246] Nigeria and Pakistan are rated as hybrid regimes, and China as authoritarian. Different strategies will be required to increase the level of democracy and human rights in each of these countries.

  - For example, during the Trump administration, the United States was downgraded from a full democracy to a flawed democracy. In 2020, the voters and the Electoral College put Trump out of office. Since then, the Biden administration, the House of Representatives' January 6 Committee, and several federal and state prosecutors have carried out a range of actions to put the country on course to recover its status as a full democracy. Whether they succeed will be determined in the 2024 and subsequent elections, and in the success of the country in putting Trump and other anti-democratic politicians and conspirators in the rear view mirror.

  - Brazil and Indonesia appear to be on track to maintain their status as partial democracies, although both countries have the potential to become full democracies in the coming years based on internal reforms and with effective economic and political support from other democratic countries.

  - Nigeria is an especially interesting case because its rapid population growth is projected to make it the second largest country in the world by 2100, with India remaining in first place and China dropping to third.[247] The World Bank ranks Nigeria in the bottom third of all countries in the world in terms of median income per person.[248] A key question is, by what means can a large, rapidly growing, poor country such as Nigeria become more democratic in the next quarter of a century? Technical and financial support from democratic countries is part of the answer. Improved access to emigration is another. Ultimately, however, free and fair elections would be the cornerstone of democratic reform in Nigeria.

- ♦ The same question can be posed about Pakistan, which is not growing nearly as fast as Nigeria, but still faces the problem of a large country with a low median income (and a high level of corruption). And the same potential answers proposed for Nigeria apply to Pakistan as well: technical and financial support from democratic countries, fair migration policies, and, most importantly, free and fair elections.

- ♦ China shows no signs of becoming a democracy in the near future, and may be turning increasingly authoritarian, as evidenced by the takeover of, and anti-democratic policies, in Hong Kong, the potential military takeover of Taiwan, and the continued persecution of Tibetans, Uyghurs, and other minorities. But, as stated above, no one can predict the future. In any case, democratic countries around the world can keep calling attention to and sanctioning China's human rights violations in hopes that, short of major democratic reforms, at least the repressive actions of the Chinese government can be reduced in the decades ahead.

Conclusion

We have covered a lot of ground in this chapter – including the importance of democracy in transitioning to a cooperative economy, the imperfect role of the United States in helping to set the stage for modern democracies, the spread of democracies in the world in the 1800s and 1900s, the gradual decline of democracy in the early 21st century, and recommendations for how democracies can be revived and expanded in the second quarter of the century.

The next chapter focuses on opportunities for increasing economic democracy by 2050.

Chapter 8

Excellent Growth Potential for Economic Democracy in the Coming Decades

Introduction

Definition and measurement of economic democracy

As referred to in this book, economic democracy is a combined measure of the strength of labor, consumer, and other civil society organizations; and of cooperatives and other democratically owned and controlled businesses.

The definition of economic democracy presented in the introduction to the book includes the following excerpt: "a shift [in] ownership and decision-making power from corporate shareholders and corporate managers (such as a board of directors) to a larger group of public stakeholders that includes workers, consumers, suppliers, communities and the broader public."[249]

Although the above excerpt focuses on the application of economic democracy to corporate boards of directors, the approach taken in this book applies the concept of economic democracy more broadly to intergovernmental organizations; national, regional, and local governments, other organizations, and actions taken by informal groups.

In some ways economic democracy is parallel to political democracy because it can be based on "free and fair voting," as in elections to the boards of directors of cooperatives, for-profit corporations, and decision making by labor unions and other membership organizations.

But in other ways, economic democracy is very different from political democracy. It involves individuals, families, and communities being in control of their everyday lives. It can include activities such as community supported agriculture (CSAs)[250] (in which community members enter into agreements to purchase food directly from local farmers), public banking, fair trade agreements (in which farmers, artisans, and small business owners in developing countries receive a larger share of the value of their production by skipping traditional international intermediaries in their relationships with consumers), as well as the more abstract labor, consumer, and other "public stakeholder" issues mentioned above.

Economic democracy also includes reforms that close various legal and regulatory loopholes that allow corporations, political groups, other organizations, and wealthy individuals to exert disproportionate influence on economic decision making. The influence occurs through false representations, the abuse of nonprofit status, minimization of tax payments, and lobbying for various political policies that favor the wealthy over the rest of us.

At the present time, there are no clear, widely agreed-upon measures of economic democracy. Thus, until such a set of measures is developed and implemented, it will not be easily possible to determine whether economic democracy is increasing or decreasing over time, or to compare levels of economic democracy across different countries, different levels of government, or within organizations. This lack of agreed-upon measures is also an impediment to evaluating whether policies and actions are effective in increasing economic democracy. Thus, it is of critical importance to develop and implement useful measures, such as those that exist for political democracy. This might be an appropriate responsibility for the UN Department of Economic and Social Affairs, which overseas the Sustainable Development Goals program.

It should be noted that there is overlap in some measures of political democracy, economic democracy, quality of life, and environmental sustainability. It is important to avoid using overlapping measures of these four components of the cooperative economy in order to avoid biased measurement results.

The categories and analyses of economic democracy presented in this chapter are intended to contribute to the development of future measures of this critically important component of the co-operative economy.

Categories of economic democracy

In this book, economic democracy is characterized by four main factors:

1. Organizations that promote the rights of "public stakeholders, including workers, consumers, suppliers, communities and the broader public"[251]

2. Laws and regulations that protect the interests of the above public stakeholders

3. For-profit businesses that are wholly or partly owned and/or controlled by employees and/or other public stakeholders

4. Cooperatives and other democratically owned and controlled businesses, the primary purposes of which are to provide services to their members

Organization of this chapter

The first three categories of economic democracy presented above are discussed in the next section of this chapter.

Because cooperatives are such a key part of economic democracy, they will receive more detailed attention in the latter part of the chapter. The roles that these member-owned business organizations are already playing in the world's economies will be described first, followed by an analysis of their potential to play an even greater role in furthering economic democracy in the decades ahead.

The roles of advocacy organizations, laws and regulations, and participation in corporate decision-making in increasing economic democracy

1
Advocacy organizations

All of us are consumers. Many of us are also workers, either in our own businesses or as employees of other businesses or organizations. Some of us are self-employed or business owners. Farmers are a special category of the self-employed and/or business owners. The issue of economic democracy applies to us in all of these capacities. Especially in political democracies, we can openly advocate for the continuation or expansion of our rights. Following are major examples of groups that engage in advocacy activities.

Labor unions

As defined by Investopedia, "A labor union is an organization formed by workers in order to negotiate for better workers' rights, including better pay, safer working conditions, and better benefits. A labor union chooses representatives to negotiate on its behalf with the employer."[252]

There are other kinds of organizations in addition to labor unions that advocate for the rights of workers. The UN's International Labor Organization "brings together governments, employers and workers of 187 member states, to set labour standards, develop policies and devise programmes promoting decent work for all women and men."[253] Many other organizations share the goal of maintaining and improving workers' rights at international, national, and local levels.[254]

Consumer organizations

Wikipedia defines consumer organizations as "advocacy groups that seek to protect people from corporate abuse like unsafe products, predatory lending, false advertising, … and pollution. Consumer organizations may operate via protests, litigation, campaigning, or lobbying."[255]

Other advocacy organizations

Three prominent kinds of other advocacy organizations that relate to economic democracy are community organizations, small business organizations, and farm organizations. They advocate for their constituents at international, national, and local levels. I will not go into detail on these organizations here. However, they need to be taken into account in any broad measure of economic democracy.

2

Laws and regulations

Many advocacy organizations seek to protect their members via laws and regulations. Examples include the National Labor Relations Board[256] in the United States and similar governmental regulatory organizations in other countries, along with consumer protection laws and various kinds of anti-trust legislation and regulation.

As reported by the Cornell Law Institute, "The Federal government oversees antitrust law and consumer protection through the Federal Trade Commission which inspects complaints of scams and fraud against businesses. States use a variety of agencies and statutes to enforce consumer protection, expanding on the Federal law in many areas."[257] Most other countries have similar laws and regulatory protections for their citizens.

3

Broader participation in for-profit corporate decision-making

One means of advocating for the rights of employees (and other public stakeholders) is to have them represented on for-profit corporate boards. Such representation is common in European Union countries.[258]

Other means of broadening the economic decision-making power of employees and other public stakeholders is profit sharing, and ownership of all or part of a for-profit business enterprise. For example, in the United States, employee stock ownership plans (ESOPs) are a means for employees to own all or part of the company they work for.[259] The same kind of ownership concept could be applied to other groups of public stakeholders.

Cooperatives, the primary driver of economic democracy today and in the decades ahead

As mentioned in chapter 6, cooperative enterprises (co-ops, for short) are a widespread alternative business form to for-profit corporations. Co-ops exist in virtually every business sector and in every country in the world. The member-owners of cooperatives can be consumers, workers, businesses and other organizations, and combinations of the above ("multi-stakeholder" co-ops). Co-ops are based on a set of principles that features democratic control and the priority of services over profits.[260] (See the Appendix on Cooperative Principals and Values.)

Measurement problems related to cooperatives

As with economic democracy in general, cooperatives face a number of measurement problems. A major underlying issue is differentiating true from "fake" co-ops. True cooperatives adhere to the values and principles referred to above. Fake cooperatives do not. There are a variety of kinds of fake cooperatives. For example:

- Some government-run organizations are referred to as cooperatives even though there is no or inadequate membership voting.
- Some cooperatives exist in name only, because governmental record-keeping may not adequately track active versus inactive co-ops.

- Some "co-ops" are established in order for individuals and groups of people to receive benefits from governments or other organizations, but in fact are not engaged in cooperative business activities.

- Some organizations call themselves co-ops, but in fact are not member-controlled. They instead carry out activities that take advantage of the people they purport to serve.

A second important measurement problem is that some government ments don't have cooperative laws and regulations, or have laws and regulations inconsistent with the International Cooperative Alliance's cooperative values and principles. Thus, in these countries, it is difficult to obtain accurate data on true cooperatives.

A third measurement problem is that intergovernmental, governmental and/or research entities generally don't engage in comprehensive, periodic analyses of the number and other characteristics of cooperatives in specific countries or across countries. Without this kind of research, it is very difficult to determine patterns of cooperative growth or decline over time and to compare cooperative performance in different geographical locations.

Several recommendations on improving cooperative measurement are presented at the end of this section of the chapter.

The role of cooperatives in exemplifying and expanding economic democracy
Despite the measurement problems described above, we do have a lot of information on historical and contemporary cooperatives. This subsection of the chapter focuses on ways to build on these cooperative accomplishments. (Many of the points raised and recommendations made in this section of the chapter are derived from the book I published in 2021 entitled *Strengthening the Cooperative Community*.[261])

Cooperatives are examples of "seeds of change" that began to proliferate in the early 1800s, not long after formally organized, for-profit corporations came into existence.[262] As discussed briefly in chapter 6, co-ops have become a prominent business form in virtually every economic sector and country in the world during the past two centuries.

Because co-ops are democratically run by their members, and are service-oriented, they have excellent potential to become an important part of the emerging cooperative world economy. This part of the chapter focuses on growth opportunities for co-ops during the next several decades.

Note that the chapter does not make the case that co-ops will replace for-profit businesses in the world economy in the 21st century but, rather, that they will become an increasingly important part of this economy, contributing significantly to its democratic character and its commitment to improving quality of life and the sustainability of the environment.

Past performance and future growth opportunities for cooperatives

With over 2.5 million cooperatives and over a billion member-owners worldwide, co-ops are already a substantial part of the world economy.[263] As the co-op community increases its proactive approaches to development, as global poverty continues to diminish, and as standards of living continue to rise, cooperatives will have an even greater impact by 2050.

The growth of co-ops will come in both large, established economic sectors, where they already have a significant presence,[264] as well as in emerging parts of the world economy.

Well-established co-op sectors include the following:

Mutual and cooperative insurance companies

More than 900 million individuals, families, and businesses are policyholders of mutual and cooperative insurance companies that provide health, property, transportation, disability, life, and other insurance coverage.[265] "Mutuals" are close cousins of cooperatives. They are also democratically controlled and service-oriented. The primary difference is that democratic decision making in mutuals is done by policyholders rather than by members. As people's incomes increase, especially in developing countries, demand will increase for these mutual and cooperative insurance services.

Financial cooperatives

Financial co-ops have an estimated 700 million memberships in countries around the world.[266] The same growth dynamic mentioned for mutual and cooperative insurance companies applies to these cooperatives.

- In addition to formally organized credit unions and other financial cooperatives, more than 10,000 microfinance institutions around the world provide credit and banking services to low-income populations. Some of these institutions operate in a democratic manner, with borrowers playing a major role in decision making, and, thus, are effectively informal co-ops. However, others do not operate democratically, and in some cases, take advantage of their participants.[267] [268] As a result of unscrupulous practices by some of these organizations, there is an important need to better regulate microfinance institutions. Nonetheless, better regulated microfinance organizations could play an important role in making financial services available to low-income individuals and communities.

Agricultural supply, marketing, and service co-ops

Farmer co-ops have about 120 million, primarily family-owned, members worldwide.[269] According to a World Bank analysis carried out in 2014, "About 78 percent of the world's poor people – close to 800 million people – live in rural areas and rely largely on farming, livestock, aquaculture and other agricultural work to put food on their plates and make a living."[270] Thus, there is tremendous potential for expansion in the agricultural co-op sector, especially in developing countries, as subsistence farmers become commercial farmers in the decades ahead.

Food co-ops

An estimated 100 million people are members of food co-ops and other kinds of consumer goods co-ops. As with the financial and insurance service organizations mentioned above, these consumer goods co-ops also have substantial growth potential in the coming decades.[271]

- Food buying clubs are informal co-ops in which small groups of friends or neighbors get together to purchase bulk goods at wholesale prices.[272] The number of such community-based clubs may also grow in the coming decades, especially to meet the needs of low-income population groups.

Energy cooperatives

Energy cooperatives have a long history in the United States, in large part due to the Federal Rural Electrification Act passed in 1936.[273] Energy co-ops have excellent international growth potential due to the fact that well over 700 million people around the world currently don't have access to electricity (more on this below).[274]

Housing cooperatives

Housing cooperatives have about 16 million member households worldwide.[275] Housing cooperatives may also experience a large increase in number, especially if their sister entities – condominiums[276] and home ownership associations[277] – are included and promoted in this sector.

All of these co-op sectors have long, successful histories.[278]

Worker co-ops

Worker co-ops have well over one million employee-owners at a global level. The number of worker co-ops is not large compared to the other kinds of co-ops mentioned above. However, both because of the proliferation of social service co-ops (see below), many of which are all or partly employee-owned, and because of increasing support in the broader co-op community, the number of worker-owned co-ops could grow exponentially in the years ahead.

The growth potential in the well-established co-op sectors referred to above – with over a billion memberships and policyholders – is only part of the story. There are also a number of emerging opportunities with tremendous potential for expansion. Following are several examples of these opportunities.

Emerging co-op development opportunities
Social service co-ops

Social service co-ops are part of the rapid, recent growth of social enterprises that provide a range of job-training, childcare, elder care, and other services. Italy, in particular, has been a pioneer in the formation of social service cooperatives – with about 11,000 of them having been formed with government assistance across the country.[279] The recent growth of social enterprises (including social service cooperatives) is most pronounced in the European Union, where they have recently been estimated to provide services to almost 14 million people, and to account for about eight percent of the European Union's gross domestic product.[280] The social service co-ops in the sector are organized both as employee-owned businesses as well as co-ops with multiple groups of members, including employees, clients, and other groups (often referred to as "multi-stakeholder" cooperatives).[281]

The Sustainable Development Goals (SDG) initiative of the United Nations

The SDG program (the successor of the Millennium Development Goals program), referred to in chapter 6, also presents growth opportunities for co-ops in the coming decades. Altogether, there are 17 SDGs with measurable objectives to be achieved by 2030.[282] Virtually all of these goals provide co-op opportunities. Several prominent examples include the following:

SDG Goal 1, No poverty, and Goal 2, Zero hunger

Agricultural and food cooperatives directly address these two goals. The 800 million poor farmers and other rural residents, cited above by the World Bank, could benefit greatly from both of these kinds of cooperatives.

- Because of the availability of joint technical assistance, purchasing, and marketing services, agricultural co-ops can play a major role in assisting subsistence farmers to become commercial farmers. As intermittent rainfall and drought conditions become an increasing challenge to farmers in some developing countries as a result of climate change, co-ops can assist farmers in carrying out "conservation agriculture" practices that reduce their vulnerability to these climate-related challenges.[283]

- As mentioned above, one of the simplest forms of food co-ops is informal food buying clubs. Small groups of people in both rural and urban settings can get together, buy items in bulk, and share them among the members at a much lower cost than purchasing by individual families. Buying clubs can evolve into more formally organized food co-ops. Cumulatively, the benefits to members can make a big difference in reducing the percentage of each family's income that goes into food and other consumer goods purchasing.

SDG Goal 3, Good health and well-being

According to Deloitte's *2023 Global Health Care Outlook*, "More than a quarter of the world's population has no access to essential medicines, and for more than 2 billion people worldwide, medicines may be unaffordable, unavailable, inaccessible, or of poor or unregulated quality."[284] Increasing healthcare access can be effectively addressed by community health cooperatives.

> *I did research on this kind of cooperative in Kenya in the first decade of the 21st century. NCBA CLUSA, a U.S.-based non-profit, helped to form hundreds of democratically organized village and multi-village health planning and implementation projects in different parts of the country. In the program, villagers identified the major health-related problems in their communities, and developed solutions to them. In some cases, they addressed health problems themselves by providing clean drinking water, improving village sanitation, and reducing the population of malaria-bearing mosquitoes. They also selected individuals from the village to receive training as basic health providers, set up local small pharmacies, and increased access to nearby health clinics. At its peak, in 2010, about two million rural Kenyans had participated in this program.[285]*

This model could be adapted in other developing countries in which villagers (and poor urban residents) lack good access to healthcare services. It's a simply structured, low-cost, self-help approach that could be organized in thousands of communities in Africa, Asia, and Latin America. Some of the reasons why healthcare and other community-based cooperatives have not been more widely developed are presented in a later section of this chapter.

SDG Goal 7, Affordable and clean energy, and Goal 13, Climate action

Community-based cooperatives are particularly well-suited to addressing these two related goals.

- Well over 700 million people, mostly in rural areas of the Global South, have no access to electricity.[286] Community solar co-ops can provide a clean energy source for lighting, heating, and cooking. But the co-ops need to be organized and financed in order for large numbers of rural residents to form and become members of them.[287]

- More than two billion people in the Global South are dependent on fossil fuels such as concentrated natural gas and kerosene, or carbon dioxide-producing wood and charcoal. All of these fuels have the additional disadvantage of creating an unhealthy, smoky atmosphere in and near households. Some of these householders have proven to be resistant to using electric cooking appliances. Community-based energy co-ops can also be a means to establish manure digesters that produce biogas and other means to produce clean biofuels to address this resistance to cooking with electricity.

- Another example of a community-based co-op with huge potential to address climate change issues is forestry and perennial grass co-ops. These co-ops can be used to improve land management, and to plant trees and grasses in areas that have been deforested as well as in non-forested areas that are favorable to the planting of trees and perennial grasses. Forestry co-ops are an important means to sequester carbon and therefore reduce the amount of carbon dioxide going into the atmosphere. These kinds of co-ops can be formed by local residents to protect and improve privately owned, communal, and state-owned land. As with community solar co-ops, the development of forestry and perennial grass co-ops requires organizing and financing.[288]

The core problems limiting international cooperative development

Despite all of the opportunities for co-op growth cited above, one main problem could interfere with their realization: The international cooperative community does not have an integrated set of organizations, networks, and services to carry out ambitious, coordinated cooperative development projects.

As mentioned in chapter 6, the International Cooperative Alliance (ICA) has been in existence for almost 135 years and has done an excellent job of establishing and growing a membership organization for "more than 310 organisations from 107 countries" representing all cooperative sectors.[289]

The key words in the above paragraph are "membership organization." As such, ICA provides educational and communication services among its members, defines and updates co-op principles and values, and promotes the cooperative model as a preferred way to do business.

But a cooperative membership organization is not the same as a cooperative development entity or network. The primary mission of a membership organization is to serve its members and not to engage actively in the expansion of existing co-ops or the formation of new ones. The following brief story illustrates this point.

The Wisconsin Federation of Cooperatives in the United States hosted a summit on cooperative development in 1982. A major conclusion of the summit was that, as a co-op membership organization, the Federation was not in the best position to actively work on the expansion of cooperatives in the state. Its primary mission was to use its membership dues to serve its existing members. The summit recommended the formation of a new entity, specifically formed to provide development services to new and established cooperatives.

I was hired by the Federation in January 1985 to take the lead in forming this new development organization. Federation staff, a steering committee of cooperative leaders, and I spent most of that year incorporating – and developing a business plan – for this new non-profit entity called the Wisconsin Cooperative Development Council. This initial work led to a grant from the State of Wisconsin matched by funding from several large cooperative organizations. We began providing co-op development services in early 1986. In 1993, the Council merged with a non-profit co-op services organization in the neighboring state of Minnesota, and also joined forces with the Iowa Institute for Cooperatives. As a result of this expansion, the Council was renamed Cooperative Development Services (CDS).

As of 2024, CDS has been in business for 38 years, assisting hundreds of co-ops to form and grow in the three-state area and beyond. The Council/CDS was the second domestically oriented cooperative development organization formed in the United States. The Federation of Southern Cooperatives was the first, and is still operating today.[290] Cooperation Works!, a national organization formed by co-op development organizations in the United States in the early 1990s, now has over 40 members serving all 50 states.[291]

The moral of this story: The best way to develop and expand the cooperative movement is through organizations and networks whose mission is to do just that. This section of the chapter makes a number of recommendations on how to create a comprehensive set of cooperative development services at the international level.

But first, another story. Following is a slightly revised version of an excerpt from my book, *Strengthening the Cooperative Community*, published in 2021.

Mondragon

"Mondragon is the most famous employee-owned cooperative federation in the world. In the 1950s, José María Arizmendiarrieta, a young Catholic priest who taught at the technical high school near the city of Mondragon in the Basque region of Spain, was the primary strategist for, and organizer of, a manufacturing business owned by its 26 employees. Over

the years, a network of additional businesses and related organizations was added to this worker co-op federation. According to Mondragon's 2018 annual report, more than 80,000 employees, almost 75% of whom were member-owners, worked for the affiliated 260 individual businesses in the co-op network.[292]

"In the 1950s, Mondragon and the rest of the Basque region were in the midst of an economic depression brought about by the Spanish Civil War and the animosity [toward the region] by the Franco regime. The co-op federation created an array of inter-related co-op businesses and service organizations that stimulated the local economy, launched successful affiliated businesses, and provided support services to local residents.

"For example, if a group wanted to form a new worker co-op, they developed a business plan with the technical support of Mondragon's business consultants. If the plan appeared feasible, it could receive financing from the co-op network's credit union. Then, the network would continue to provide technical assistance to the new worker co-op to increase the likelihood that it would be successful. Not only that, the co-op network has a technical school that provides well-trained employees for its co-op member companies. If there are layoffs in one of the businesses, the network reassigns the unemployed workers to other businesses or to further training, followed by re-employment in a network business."[293]

There have been recent challenges faced by Mondragon since I wrote the above excerpt. As with other businesses around the world, the COVID pandemic created significant problems for the Federation. A number of its member businesses faced financial difficulties. This, in turn, resulted in two major businesses – Ulma Group and Orona Cooperative – voting to leave the Federation in December 2022. The primary cause of the rift was that both co-ops wanted more autonomy. The combined number of employees of the two organizations is 11,000, almost 15% of Mondragon's total workforce. Plans continue for some joint activities between Mondragon and the two co-ops. Nonetheless, their departure represents a blow to the Federation.[294]

The primary take-away from this example is Mondragon's model of integrated development. For more than 70 years, Mondragon has developed and implemented a highly successful system for establishing and maintaining co-op businesses. The recent departure of two major organizations over the issue of autonomy may bring about restructuring in the future, but that does not negate the value of Mondragon's development approach.

Clearly, a difference exists between the development strategy of one, mostly regionally based, co-op federation and the international cooperative movement. But there are similarities as well. As I point out in *Strengthening the Cooperative Community*, basic building blocks for developing individual co-ops and networks of co-ops include entrepreneurship, research, education, technical and organizational support, laws and regulations, financing, and cooperation among cooperatives, plus the integration of these building blocks.[295]

Mondragon has done a brilliant job of bringing these development components together. The international cooperative community has not yet done so. But it can. And, if it does, the growth of successful cooperatives will explode in the coming decades.

Recommendations for international co-op development reforms

In *Strengthening the Cooperative Community*, I make several recommendations for filling the gaps in the provision for, and coordination of, cooperative development building blocks at the international level. Following is a consolidated presentation of some of the key recommendations.

1. *Establish a formal network of international cooperative development organizations.* In the United States, about 10 such organizations already coordinate their activities through the US Overseas Cooperative Development Council.[296] There are also approximately 10 European internationally oriented cooperative development organizations that coordinate some of their activities.[297] Canada and a scattering of countries in the Global South also have internationally oriented development organizations, although there is an acute need for many more such organizations in developing countries. It would not be a big step to create a formal network among these organizations.

2. *Establish an international cooperative development foundation.* The International Cooperative Alliance or another grouping of co-op organizations should designate a task force to take the lead in forming an international cooperative development foundation or network of foundations. Three critical steps in launching such a foundation would be to:

   - Select an interim board of directors/fundraising committee composed of representatives from a diverse array of co-op sectors and regions
   - Develop an appropriate legal structure for the foundation or network of foundations
   - Hire a professional fundraising firm to help design a solicitation strategy; conduct a survey of the CEOs and managers of major co-ops, foundations, governmental development organizations (such as USAID), and other potential donors; and secure commitments of financial support from them

A successful international cooperative development program will require a well-funded, financially secure, and well-staffed organization dedicated to that purpose.

3. *Form cooperative business planning networks.* These networks could be supported in part by the foundation, and would consist of cooperative development organizations, business and financial planners, and others knowledgeable about co-op

development growth opportunities. The networks would identify, prioritize, implement, and support specific co-op business initiatives.

- ◆ Cooperatives very rarely develop themselves. To turn ideas into successful co-op businesses requires research, careful planning, financing, a start-up strategy, and ongoing support and monitoring. Cooperative business planning networks can help coordinate all of these components.

4. *Develop an international cooperative financial network.* This financial network would closely coordinate with the business planning networks described above. In addition to providing direct loans and other financial support, members of the network would also provide loan guarantees and partial loan guarantees to credit unions and other lenders in order to reduce their risks.

- ◆ As we saw above, thousands of existing financial cooperatives and other public and private banking institutions can participate individually and/or jointly in financing the development and expansion of cooperatives. An international cooperative financial network can help address the key problem of coordination among these organizations in investing in co-op development.

5. *Assist in the organization of additional cooperative development organizations.* An important complement to the above recommendation is increasing the number and level of expertise of cooperative development organizations in both developing and developed countries.

- ◆ As mentioned above, a few dozen of these organizations already exist, mostly located in developed countries, but the general lack of this kind of entity, especially in developing countries, impedes co-op growth where both the need and the opportunities are the greatest.

6. *Do a better job of measuring the performance of cooperatives as individual businesses and at national and international levels.* This can be accomplished in large part through better coordination among co-op researchers, developers, and new and established

co-ops. This coordination can be facilitated through the business planning networks.

- Co-ops increase their likelihood of survival and growth when they have access to practical, applied research, whether it's market analysis, performance auditing and evaluation, or case studies that provide lessons for other co-ops.
- A lack of comparative, longitudinal analyses of cooperatives at the national and international levels is a serious detriment to understanding and improving co-op performance by learning from the experience of peer organizations and applying lessons learned over time. Euricse (the European Union Research Institute on Cooperatives and Social Enterprises), mentioned in chapter 6, is particularly well-suited to conducting worldwide censuses of cooperatives every five years to help fill this void.
- Many researchers and research institutions focus on cooperatives. Most of these are located in developed countries. The Committee on Cooperative Research and the Cooperative Law Committee are coordinated through the International Cooperative Alliance. However, not much of this research is targeted to assisting in the development and operation of co-ops and to solving the problems they face.
- As with the cooperative financial network mentioned above, applied research on co-ops should be coordinated through cooperative business planning networks and cooperative development organizations.

The expansion and improved coordination of – and development assistance to – cooperatives around the world is a key part of transitioning to a more cooperative economy in the coming decades.

The good news is that millions of co-ops and more than a billion co-op members are already in place. We know the model works, and that many opportunities are available for expanding the size and number of these co-ops.

The less-good news is that there is a need for much greater coordination among cooperative development organizations – and for cooperative development fundraising, planning, organizing, financial networking, and applied research – to realize the potential for exponential growth in the decades ahead.

Conclusion

This chapter presents major definitional and measurement issues related to economic democracy, provides information on advocacy organizations and laws and regulations related to economic democracy, and describes ways in which workers and representatives of other public interest groups can be represented in corporate decision making. The primary focus of the latter part of the chapter is on expanding the role of cooperatives in the world economy during the next several decades.

The next chapter describes and analyzes the role of quality of life as a component of the cooperative world economy.

Chapter 9

Improving Quality of Life in the Decades Ahead

Introduction

Improving quality of life around the world and building a cooperative economy are inextricably linked. Our current world economy is characterized by extreme inequality within and between countries, and by the concentration of wealth and power among a small percentage of the world's population.

According to "Survival of the Richest," an Oxfam Briefing Paper, published in January 2023, "Over the last 10 years, the richest 1% of humanity has captured more than half of all new global wealth. Since 2020, according to Oxfam analysis of Credit Suisse data, this wealth grab by the super-rich has accelerated, and the richest 1% have captured almost two-thirds of all new wealth. This is six times more than the bottom 90% of humanity. Since 2020, for every dollar of new global wealth gained by someone in the bottom 90%, one of the world's billionaires has gained $1.7m."[298]

The connection between wealth and quality of life is obvious. With enough money, one can purchase the goods and services necessary to survive and prosper. In some parts of the world, even poor people have access to basic goods and services through governmental and nongovernmental programs. In most places they don't.

Humans (and other species) need to meet our basic needs in order to survive or we would become extinct. On the other end of the spectrum, having a good quality of life means that we are not just meeting our basic needs but living well, with surpluses that allow us to enjoy life, have leisure time, and be creative.

Some of us live in families and communities that already have surplus goods, services, and time, but the large majority of us do not. In a cooperative economy, a primary goal would be that all of us would have a high quality of life.

In the first half of the 21st century, we have the means for every human being on the planet to have a decent quality of life. The primary problem is one of distribution rather than adequacy of resources. Reducing the extreme inequality in wealth and income around the world is thus one of the primary means to provide an adequate quality of life for all of us.

Definition and measurement of quality of life

A variety of approaches can be used to define quality of life. The World Bank cites its primary goal as "working for a world free of poverty,"[299] with poverty defined as "a lack of basic human needs, such as food, water, shelter, freedom, access to education, healthcare, or employment. … In other words, poverty is defined as a low quality of life."[300] That is the primary definition used in this chapter.

There are several advantages to using this approach to define quality of life:

- Poverty and wealth are key measures of an individual's, family's, or community's ability to survive and prosper. In general, the more resources and/or access to basic services one has, the better the quality of one's life.

- We can debate specific items on the quality-of-life list, but the underlying premise is that humans need a minimal set of conditions in order to survive. Usually at or near the top of this list are food, water, shelter,.… [and] access to education, healthcare, or employment. Freedom and democracy are also important, but a majority of the people in the world today don't have access to them, and yet, get by.

- Poverty is measurable over time, in different countries and at different levels of society. So also are quality-of-life components (such as those listed in the above paragraph). This means that we can see progress (or regress) in reducing (or failing to reduce) poverty as a whole as well as for each quality-of-life component.

- One dimension that should be added to this list is the inter-generational transfer of the quality of life. *Our Common Future,* also known as *The Brundtland Report,* was published in 1987 by the United Nations. The report defines sustainable development as development that "meets the needs of the present without compromising the ability of future generations to meet their own needs."[301] Put more crassly: What's the point of having one generation live with abundance only to have the next generation have a reduced quality of life?

Amassing goodies is not the path to a good quality of life

The ability to collect luxury items is a lousy definition of quality of life as the Beatles remind us in their 1964 hit "Can't Buy Me Love."[302]

As the title of the song suggests, one can't buy love or happiness or the good life. However, recent research in the United States does show that to a certain extent, the amount of money one earns does correlate with increased happiness.[303] One of the authors of the study commented that, "Money is not the secret to happiness, but it can probably help a bit." Note that the study did not look at the super-rich, so there may very well be a point after which additional wealth does not correlate with a higher quality of life.

Sense of community

A much different view emphasizes that many aspects of quality of life come from our relationships with others, not from material objects or access to services such as education and healthcare. There is a large body of literature on "sense of community," one definition of which is "a feeling that members have of belonging, a feeling that members matter to one another and to the group, and a shared faith that members' needs will be met through commitment to be together."[304]

The *Animalia* website defines social animals as "those. ... that interact highly with other animals. ... to the point of having a recognizable and distinct society. They associate in social groups and form cooperative societies."[305]

Humans and other primates are social animals. From our very beginnings, modern humans *(Homo sapiens)* lived in small groups. Our core identity as a species involves the sense of community we had (and have) in these groups. Thus, quality of life is inextricably tied to the communities in which we live, work, and play.

If this sense-of-community perspective is over-emphasized, however, then we fail to give adequate attention to the fact that basic access to food, clothing, housing, etc., is also essential to having a good quality of life. Thus, one could argue that there are two main dimensions to quality of life: having enough food and other resources to sustain life, and having a sense of community that makes life worth living.

A general premise of this book is that goals and objectives need to be measurable in order to be useful. With that premise in mind, both a sense of community and the physical and service resources described above are measurable traits related to quality of life.

Measuring a sense of community

A number of measures of sense of community have been used by social scientists during the past four decades or so.[306] They generally take the form of indices in which people rate their psychological sense of community. For example, one index measures four dimensions of sense of community: membership, influence, reinforcement of needs, and shared emotional connection.[307] These indices have been applied at the neighborhood level, in schools, and in a variety of other social settings.

It would be possible, but probably not very useful, to develop an index or set of indices that could be applied to urban and rural communities around the world. The question is: What would be the purpose of such an ambitious measurement initiative? Of more relevance to the goals of this book would be measures of efficacy in strengthening positive senses of community at local and multi-local levels. For example, one community health project I evaluated in Kenya in the early 2000s was very successful in mobilizing several thousand villages to take positive, self-help steps to improve their quality of health.[308] Applied research on these kinds of projects is directly related to improving quality of life in participating villages as well as in providing lessons for other communities.

Although sense of community is an important aspect of quality of life, I will not emphasize it in this chapter because it is best used as a means to measure and improve sense of community at the local level, and not as a broad, comparative tool.

Measurement of goods and services that improve quality of life

The World Bank quote cited above provides a fairly comprehensive list of key components of a decent quality of life, focusing on eliminating extreme poverty in the world.

In this chapter, the Millennium Development Goals (MDG) program facilitated by the United Nations between 2000 and 2015[309] and the Sustainable Development Goals (SDG) program, begun in 2016 and ending in 2030,[310] exemplify quality-of-life initiatives that have clear, measurable objectives and have been endorsed by virtually all of the countries in the world.

An evaluation of performance on these quality-of-life goals is the focus of a later section of this chapter.

Organization of the chapter

As with chapters 7, 8, and 10, this chapter is divided into two main sections: historical trends in quality of life and the other components of a cooperative economy, and strategies for improvement in the future.

Trends in quality of life around the world

It's tricky to reach back 300,000 years, 12,000 years, 5,000 years, or even 250 years and try to determine what our quality of life as humans was around each of these times, although some clues exist. However, much of what our lives were like then is largely a matter of speculation. That won't stop me from doing some retrospective analysis, but I won't dwell too much on the distant past and instead will primarily focus on the 20th and early 21st centuries.

As presented in chapter 1, we can get some sense of what human lives were like at the dawn of our species by looking at the lives of chimpanzees today. Ignoring for the moment the fact that chimpanzees are an endangered species because of threats created by humans, life is pretty good for many groups of chimps in the wild. They have enough to eat. In most cases, their health is good. They generally get along with each other – playing, gathering food, and hunting together – although in some troops, dominant males and females may make life uncomfortable for others by their overbearing behavior. Sometimes there are clashes among different groups of chimps. Their life span in the wild is about 33 years.[311] The last common ancestor that humans had with chimpanzees lived about 6 million to 7 million years ago.[312] Chimpanzees have been around far longer than modern humans. This is a testament to their ability to survive as a species.

The above paragraph probably does a pretty good job of describing "modern human" life before we settled down and began farming. Differences between the species are that we modern humans walked on our hind legs, and therefore were better adapted to live in open areas and had greater geographical mobility. Walking on two legs also gave us the ability to use our forelimbs to hold, manipulate, and throw objects.

Other differences between the two species are lesser dependency by humans on trees for nesting and on edible fruits for our diets, and our greater ability to protect ourselves from other animals, thus making it easier for us to survive and move from place to place. Not long after our emergence as a species about 300,000 years ago, we had spread across many parts of Africa. Beginning about 90,000 years ago, we had ventured into the Middle East and southern Asia.

Chapter 3 describes our transition from hunting and gathering to farming that began about 12,000 years ago. Again, there is much speculation about why we made this transition, but the predominant explanations are that a drying and warming climate limited animals that could be hunted and other food that could be gathered. Increasing population density may also have been a factor in our settling down and farming as a means to meet our food needs without having to compete or conflict with other groups of humans – at least in the early days of agriculture.

In any case, humans in most parts of the world became primarily dependent on agriculture for their food between 12,000 and 5,000 years ago. What does this mean for our quality of life? As Israeli historian Yuval Noah Harari[313] and other authors have concluded, there were pluses and minuses. Because we were producing most of it ourselves, our food security increased. But there is evidence that the quality of our diets worsened because of overdependence on grains.[314] Also, because we lived in closer proximity, the likelihood of passing diseases to one another increased, as did the frequency of conflict within and between communities. So, some scientists have argued that our quality of life deteriorated as a result of the transition from hunting and gathering to agriculture.

For example, as Harari put it, "Foragers knew the secrets of nature long before the Agricultural Revolution, since their survival depended on an intimate knowledge of the animals they hunted and the plants they gathered. Rather than heralding a new era of easy living, the Agricultural Revolution left farmers with lives generally more difficult and less satisfying than those of foragers. Hunter-gatherers spent their time in more stimulating and varied ways and were less in danger of starvation and disease. The Agricultural Revolution certainly enlarged the sum total of food at the disposal of humankind, but the extra food did not translate into a better diet or more leisure. Rather it translated into population explosions and pampered elites. The average farmer worked harder than the average forager and got a worse diet in return. The Agricultural Revolution was history's biggest fraud."[315]

And for most people, quality of life probably got even worse during the past 5,000 years. On the positive side, we continued to improve our ability to meet our needs for food security and shelter and to make a wide array of tools (including weapons). On the negative side, our population size grew and required us to live in greater proximity to one another in villages, cities, city-states, tribes, and empires. This, in turn, led to increasingly hierarchical societies, greater inequality in the distribution of wealth, more rapid spread of diseases, and more conflict within and between groups of humans.

Then along came the Industrial Revolution beginning about 250 years ago. In this relatively short span of time, our ability to invent "labor-saving" devices, mechanize our work lives, and more radically alter our environment increased rapidly. We began to live in a much more global society, dominated by European empires. Some people had levels of luxury that could never have been dreamed of in earlier times. But, despite the emergence of a few democratic countries, there was also extreme inequality – including slavery, servitude, and other forms of political and economic oppression that made most of our lives worse, not better.

The 20th century was a roller coaster. These hundred years marked the end of the European imperial era. Two world wars and a worldwide depression made it clear that modern empires did not hold the key to a sustainable quality of life in the first half of the century. In the second half, former colonies became countries, but were still subject to exploitation by a handful of dominant European countries and corporations. Most of the inhabitants of these nation-states continued (and continue) to have a low quality of life, in part because of exploitation by outsiders, but also as a result of rule by self-serving, domestic elites.

The beginning of the end of extreme poverty

A positive turning point began in mid-century after the end of World War II. In response to the severe economic uncertainty and carnage precipitated during the first half of the century, most countries in the world were ready to try a more peaceful and economically secure world paradigm. The primary means for turning this momentous corner was the formation of the United Nations in 1945.

Following is an excerpt from the preamble to the UN charter.

"We the peoples of the United Nations determined: to save succeeding generations from the scourge of war, which twice in our lifetime has brought untold sorrow to mankind, and to reaffirm faith in fundamental human rights, in the dignity and worth of the human person, in the equal rights of men and women and of nations large and small, and to establish conditions under which justice and respect for the obligations arising from treaties and other sources of international law can be maintained, and to promote social progress and better standards of life in larger freedom,

> *"And for these ends: to practice tolerance and live together in
> peace with one another as good neighbours, and to unite our
> strength to maintain international peace and security, and
> to ensure, by the acceptance of principles and the institution
> of methods, that armed force shall not be used, save in the
> common interest, and to employ international machinery for
> the promotion of the economic and social advancement of
> all peoples..."[316]*

This preamble reads like a declaration of human rights for the world. This doesn't mean that all the "bad guy" countries suddenly saw the light of freedom and human rights, but it did mean that the rulers of these countries were willing to sign a document alleging that they believed in these rights and were willing to be part of a new, integrated world organization dedicated to implementing them.

So, here we are at the end of the first quarter of the 21st century. Has quality of life for most people improved much in the past three-quarters of a century? Probably not. But there are signs that we may be on the verge of such a change.

The seeds of change referred to in chapter 6 have begun to improve quality of life in some parts of the world. And, despite the perceived intractability of major world problems, such as extreme poverty, inequality, and the crises precipitated by human-caused climate change, we have begun to make halting steps toward addressing these problems.

The MDGs and the SDGs: measuring recent trends in quality of life

The UN's eight Millennium Development Goals (MDGs) were intended to radically improve quality of life around the world by eliminating extreme poverty and hunger, achieving universal primary education, promoting empowerment of women, accomplishing a range of health objectives (including major reductions in child mortality, maternal mortality, HIV/AIDS, malaria, tuberculosis, and other diseases), and promoting environmental sustainability.

The MDG goals were expanded to 17 Sustainable Development Goals (SDGs) in 2016 with the addition of water, sanitation, and energy goals; economic growth, employment, and other development goals; climate change goals; and goals related to marine and terrestrial ecosystems.

Both sets of goals have measurable objectives that are analyzed each year for almost every country and region in the world.

As stated at the beginning of the chapter, I use the measurements developed for the MDGs and SDGs as the primary means of assessing whether the quality of the lives of people around the world has improved since the beginning of the 21st century.

The Millennium Development Goals: 2000-2015

"The United Nations Millennium Declaration, signed in September 2000, commits world leaders to combat poverty, hunger, disease, illiteracy, environmental degradation, and discrimination against women.… Each MDG has targets set for 2015 and indicators to monitor progress from 1990 levels."[317]

What's notable about these goals is that they aren't just a set of platitudes about making the world a better place to live. They are backed up by measurable objectives and a specific time frame. Not all of the goals were achieved by 2015, but many were, and significant progress was made on those goals that weren't fully achieved.

Following is a review of achievements related to the eight MDG goals summarized in *The Millennium Development Goals Report 2015*:[318]

- "Globally, the number of people living in extreme poverty has declined by more than half, falling from 1.9 billion in 1990 to 836 million in 2015. Most progress has occurred since 2000…

- "The number of out-of-school children of primary school age worldwide has fallen by almost half, to an estimated 57 million in 2015, down from 100 million in 2000…

- "Many more girls are now in school compared to [2000]. The developing regions as a whole have achieved the target to eliminate gender disparity in primary, secondary and tertiary education. …

- "The global under-five mortality rate has declined by more than half, dropping from 90 to 43 deaths per 1,000 live births between 1990 and 2015…

- "Since 1990, the maternal mortality ratio has declined by 45 per cent worldwide, and most of the reduction has occurred since 2000…

- "New HIV infections fell by approximately 40 per cent between 2000 and 2013, from an estimated 3.5 million cases to 2.1 million. …

- "Over 6.2 million malaria deaths have been averted between 2000 and 2015, primarily of children under five years of age in sub-Saharan Africa…

- "Between 2000 and 2013, tuberculosis prevention, diagnosis and treatment interventions saved an estimated 37 million lives. …

- "Globally, 147 countries have met the drinking water target, 95 countries have met the sanitation target and 77 countries have met both. …

- "Official development assistance from developed countries increased by 66 per cent in real terms between 2000 and 2014, reaching $135.2 billion."

Mixed results for the UN's Sustainable Development Goals program

Unlike the dramatic improvements reported for the MDGs, the SDG program has not fared so well. *The Sustainable Development Goals Report 2023*[319] presents the following evaluation:

"Halfway to the deadline for the 2030 Agenda. … we are leaving more than half the world behind. Progress on more than 50 per cent of targets of the SDGs is weak and insufficient; on 30 per cent, it has stalled or gone into reverse. These include key targets on poverty, hunger and climate. Unless we act now, the 2030 Agenda could become an epitaph for a world that might have been.

"The COVID-19 pandemic and the triple crises of climate change, biodiversity loss and pollution are having a devastating and lasting impact. This has been amplified by Russia's invasion of Ukraine, which has driven increases in the prices of food and energy and in the cost of access to finance, creating a global cost-of-living crisis affecting billions of people.

"The SDGs are the universally-agreed road map to bridge economic and geopolitical divides, restore trust and rebuild solidarity. Failure to make progress means inequalities will continue to deepen, increasing the risk of a fragmented, two-speed world. No country can afford to see the 2030 Agenda fail."[320]

Given the generally weak performance in accomplishing the SDGs to date, we are in danger of experiencing just such a failure.

The impacts of population change and migration on quality of life

Before turning to the positive changes that could take place during the next quarter century, I need to add a pair of complications to the equation: population change and migration. If these two closely linked phenomena are not addressed with urgency as we attempt to improve quality of life around the world, we will subject ourselves to a much more difficult and prolonged path to success.

This is where the concept of "sustainable development" comes into play. As stated above, quality of life needs to be passed on from one generation to the next. Climate change is a good example of past and current generations potentially undermining quality of life for future generations. (These problems will be discussed in detail in chapter 10.) Following is a presentation on how population change and migration during the next several decades will radically affect our children and grandchildren.

Population change

The growth or decline of the world's population is an important factor related to the intergenerational transfer of quality of life. Having too few people, especially those in the workforce, would threaten our survival because there would not be a significant margin of goods and services to fend off catastrophic events. For example, a pandemic or world war could tip us over the edge to a radical decline in quality of life, or even extinction. Such extinctions, in fact, have happened to all of the other 20 or so human species.[321]

On the other end of the scale, if there are too many of us, we could tax the planet's ability to meet our food, water, and other needs, and thus potentially increase human suffering and conflict, resulting in a plummeting of the world's population.

So, what's our population trajectory now? Scientists differ on the answer to this question. The United Nations Population Division recently estimated that the number of humans in the world will increase to about 10.4 billion by 2100, level off, and then start to decrease gradually.[322] In contrast, the Institute for Health Metrics and Evaluation (IHME) projects a very different population trend for the remainder of the century, with the number of people peaking at about 9.7 billion in 2064 and then shrinking to 8.8 billion by the end of the century. IHME even has a lower growth scenario that projects a decline to 6.3 billion by 2100.[323]

What's the reason for these divergent predictions? The primary difference is that IHME demographers estimate lower birth rates than the UN Population Division due primarily to increased education about, and use of, birth control in developing countries.

I lean toward the projections of the IHME researchers. In addition to increased birth control knowledge and access, there is a phenomenon referred to as the "demographic transition," in which people usually have fewer children as their quality of life improves.[324] [325] Add to these factors the already-shrinking populations in a number of countries, especially in Asia and Europe, and we appear to be heading for a lower population level in 2100 than predicted by the United Nations.

Keep in mind that education about, and access to, birth control is not just something that happens randomly. Education and access can be strongly influenced by public policy and private initiatives. Given these assumptions, I don't think a worldwide population explosion or implosion is likely during the remainder of our century, and thus will not be a primary cause of a decrease in our quality of life.

Migration

Demographers project not only the size of the population during the 21st century, but its distribution as well. For example, IHME predicts that South Korea's population will decrease from 53 million to 27 million between 2017 and 2100. During the same time period, Nigeria's population is expected to grow from 206 million to 791 million.[326]

Many other countries and regions of the world show similar imbalances. What's the solution? The most obvious one is that some of the people in countries with dense populations should migrate to countries that are declining in population.

This is easier said than done. Three of the biggest factors that exacerbate the problem of population imbalance are inconsistent migration policies from country to country, the decisions of migrants about where they would like to live, and differing cultural views about immigration. For example, South Korea and Japan have very restrictive immigration policies and low percentages of inhabitants who have moved to these countries from other parts of the world.

An international strategy on population change and migration

An international strategy is urgently needed, both to ease the current border chaos in Central and North America, the Middle East, Europe, and some parts of Asia, and to prepare for the even more extreme pressures on migration in the coming decades.

Strategies for improving quality of life between now and 2050

This section of the chapter presents a few strategies for improving quality of life in the second quarter of the 21st century, and the related goals of reducing wealth and income inequality.

In this book, the primary quality of life goal to be achieved by 2050 is that the large majority of humans are not only meeting their basic needs for survival, but also have surpluses that allow them to enjoy life, have leisure time, and be creative. Measures related to this goal should be based on human development objectives established and evaluated by the United Nations and other international bodies, and on increasing people's sense of community in the of local places in which we live around the world.

Despite the setbacks during the past few years in improving quality of life, major opportunities exist for making significant progress by mid-century. Following are seven key recommendations that can help make this happen:

1. Taxes, taxes, taxes

2. Improve economic development aid to developing countries

3. Expand the use of international and domestic wealth transfer programs, including child development accounts

4. Develop and implement an international strategy on population change and migration

5. Recommit to achieving the Sustainable Development Goals

6. Design and implement a third UN development goals program for 2031 to 2050

7. Develop and implement a range of programs that promote and contribute to a positive sense of community in urban and rural places around the world

1

Taxes, taxes, taxes

There are so many ways wealthy individuals and corporations underpay their fair share of taxes. Internationally, the wealthy and corporations are paying far lower taxes than they were just a few decades ago.[327] Following are some of the most prominent ways that countries and groups of countries could get more tax money from the rich and from large corporations, and, in turn, use some of these funds to reduce worldwide inequality and provide a decent quality of life for everyone on the planet.

- *Make tax systems more progressive.* Many countries, including the United States, used to generate a much higher percentage of federal income from progressive income taxes (the higher your income, the higher the percentage of that income you pay in taxes) than they do today.[328] In the past several decades, national income taxes have become flatter, and sales and value-added taxes make up a much larger proportion of most countries' tax systems. This means that poor and middle-income people are paying higher taxes overall than they used to. This is especially burdensome when a high proportion of one's income is spent on lodging, food, and other basic necessities. Thus, flat taxes are effectively regressive because they take up a larger portion of the disposable income of those least able to afford it.

  Since progressive taxation is popular among the majority of voters in democracies around the world,[329] they can elect political parties and leaders that commit to making taxation more progressive. That happened in the election of Biden as president and a Democratic senate in 2020 in the United States. Unfortunately, a Republican majority in the House of Representatives has blocked efforts to enact progressive taxation reform during Biden's first term. We'll see what happens in 2024.

- *Eliminate a myriad of loopholes and tax breaks and punish tax cheats.* Corporations and wealthy individuals have used their lobbying power and accountants in recent decades to reduce the amount of taxes they pay. Effective tax reform will require that taxes be progressive, but also that the numerous loopholes and tax breaks for those with the most money be eliminated, and that tax laws are rigorously enforced. Insidious ways to get around paying taxes exist in countries all over the world. Just as with progressive taxation, electorates in each country will need to elect political parties and leaders that enforce fair tax payments.

- *Enact taxes on wealth.* For the most part, countries tax income and profits, not wealth. But the major source of inequality in society is wealth, not income. The increasing concentration of wealth is primarily a function of the greater return on the investment of wealth compared to income generated by working.[330] That is, wealth begets more wealth.

The best way to break this cycle of increasing economic concentration is to tax wealth itself. A variety of experiments have been conducted in different countries around the world to implement wealth taxes. These efforts have had mixed results. During the 2020 election, Elizabeth Warren and others raised the idea of enacting a wealth tax in the United States.[331] Even though there are potential difficulties in designing and implementing effective wealth taxes, lessons learned from previous and current efforts to enact and enforce these taxes should be a priority in the coming decades.

Estate and inheritance taxes are relatively simple means to increase taxes on wealth.[332]

- *Eliminate the boondoggles, windfall taxes, tax havens, and subsidies of corporations and the wealthy.* One of the primary goals of large corporations and many wealthy individuals and families is to minimize their tax payments. As a result of lobbying power, complex accounting maneuvers, and operating on a world stage, many corporations and wealthy individuals and families have plenty of opportunities to avoid or reduce their taxes.

In February 2023, a Reuters news article reported that "In the deepest overhaul of cross-border tax rules in a generation, nearly 140 countries had agreed in 2021 to apply a minimum tax rate of 15% on multinationals by committing to a top-up tax on profits booked in countries that have lower rates."[333] The European Union is taking the lead in operationalizing this international tax agreement, which is intended to go into effect in 2024. One result of this minimum tax rate program will be to greatly reduce the ability of corporations to shop around in order to report profits from a country or group of countries that subjects them to the least amount of taxes.[334]

In an early May 2024 "Opinion – Guest Essay" in the New York Times, Gabriel Zucman, proposed a similar international tax on billionaires. Based on a 2% annual wealth tax on the 3,000 or so billionaires in the world, "…the proposal would allow countries to collect an estimated $250 billion in additional tax revenue per year, which is even more than what the global minimum tax on corporations is expected to add."[335]

2

Improve economic development aid to developing countries

In many cases, economic aid to developing countries from developed countries is based on what's good for the lender or donor rather than the recipient. At the same time, there is often inadequate accountability on the part of recipient countries to make sure that the funds received are being used as intended and with a minimum of corruption.[336]

- Two key issues here are that developing countries should have a stronger say in the assistance they receive, and that there should be accountability systems in place to ensure that the funds are spent as intended.

3
Expand the use of international and domestic wealth transfer programs, including child development accounts and other asset-building programs

Taxation isn't the only way to redistribute wealth. Other examples include a variety of kinds of profit-sharing, minimum wage laws, social and health benefits, free or subsidized public education, social security and unemployment insurance payments, negative income taxes (people below a certain income level receiving payments rather than paying income taxes),[337] and more.[338]

- Child development accounts (CDAs) are a good example of an asset-building program. One prominent approach was pioneered by the Center for Social Development at Washington University in St. Louis. CDAs "are savings or investment accounts that begin as early as birth. In many cases, public and private matching funds are deposited into these accounts to supplement savings for the child. The goal of CDAs is to promote savings and asset building for lifelong development. Thus, CDAs may be targeted to post-secondary education for youth, and home ownership and enterprise development in adulthood."[339]

CDA projects have been developed in the United States and in other countries. "The vision for CDAs has been for a universal and progressive policy aimed at long-term asset building for all." A basic goal is to bring CDAs to scale at national levels – "to all newborns in families across the full socioeconomic and geographic (rural and urban) spectrum – in a sustainable way [based on a]. … sound policy structure."

The Center for Social Development's frequently asked questions webpage reports that "There is evidence that assets, distinct from income, contribute positively to well-being. Research suggests that assets:

- Promote economic household stability and educational attainment
- Decrease the risk of intergenerational poverty transmission
- Increase health and satisfaction among adults
- Increase local civic involvement"[340]

A CDA program in Kazakhstan

Staff members of the Center for Social Development described the proposed project in mid-2023: "The National Fund of the Republic of Kazakhstan is a repository for the nation's natural-resource revenue and associated investment returns. Under the new policy announced by the president, 50% of the National Fund's annual income from natural resources will be allocated to a new National Fund for Children, which will support universal child accounts.

"Starting in January 2024, the government of Kazakhstan will automatically open an account for every child who is a citizen of Kazakhstan. Opened shortly after the beneficiary's birth, each account will receive an annual deposit from the Fund for Children until the beneficiary turns 18. … Deposits and earnings in the accounts will not be taxed, and the assets will remain inaccessible until the beneficiary reaches age 18. … After that point, the assets may be spent on education and education-related fees in Kazakhstan or overseas, or on improving a housing situation."[341]

The Center notes that, in addition to Kazakhstan, there are about 80 other resource-rich developing countries capable of financing similar programs.[342]

4

An international strategy on population change and migration

See the section above on population change and migration.

- Note, in particular, the need to develop an international policy on migration, the importance of targeting migration to countries with the highest levels of labor shortages, and the importance of reducing opposition to immigration in countries most in need of additional labor.

5

Recommit to achieving the Sustainable Development Goals

As summarized above in *The Sustainable Development Goals Report 2023*,[343] most countries in the world have dropped the ball during the past few years in their efforts to participate actively in the SDG program. Based on the success of the Millennium Development Goals in the first 15 years of this century, we know that this kind of international, coordinated approach to improving quality of life can have huge, positive outcomes in a relatively short period of time. So the issue confronting us now is: How do we get back on track in achieving as many quality-of-life goals as possible by 2030?

- *The Sustainable Development Goals Report 2023* provides some answers to this question. "First and foremost, the international community must move forward on our proposed SDG Stimulus, to scale up affordable long-term financing for all countries in need…"

  "Developing countries should have proportionate voice and representation in global decision-making institutions and processes. Economic and financial decisions should prioritize the well-being of people and planet. Governments and the private sector should reorient their economies towards low-carbon, resilient patterns of growth.

"This report calls for ambitious national benchmarks to eradicate poverty and reduce inequality, focusing on key areas: Expanding social protection and decent jobs; tackling the crisis in education; addressing gender inequality; and improving digital inclusion. These shifts must be supported by strengthened national institutions, greater accountability, effective regulatory frameworks and stronger digital infrastructure and data capacity.

"All of this requires strengthened multilateral cooperation and support for the United Nations development system. Most of all, it requires ambitious, decisive, committed action."[344]

6

Design and implement a third UN development goals program for 2031 to 2050
Even with a renewed commitment by the members of the United Nations, as described above, many of the 17 SDG goals will not be met by 2030. Thus, a third generation of UN development goals should be carefully designed and carried out between 2031 and 2050. Initiatives of this magnitude take time to research and plan, so the best time to begin this preparation is now.

Following are several recommendations for the UN's next-generation development goals program:

- Learn from the positive and negative lessons of the MDG and SDG programs and apply lessons learned to the next-generation program

- Consolidate the number of goals and targets in the program. (The sheer number of SDG goals and targets is daunting and distracting.)

- Clearly prioritize next-generation goals based on the world's projected development needs during the 2031-2050 time period
- Design the program so that it can be modified along the way to meet changing needs
- Establish sustainable financial support for implementing the new program's goals
- Reduce international, governmental, organizational, and individual corruption to ensure that financial investments in the new program's goals are not siphoned off by unscrupulous intermediaries
- Establish and enforce a clear set of negative consequences for those organizations and individuals who are caught engaging in corruption
- Follow the money, then redistribute some of it (for example, an increased transfer of funds from the Global North to the Global South); increase corporate and billionaire taxes (especially fossil fuel-related earnings); establish multilateral development banks, other financial institutions, nonprofit organizations, and other sources of funding for the next-generation program
- Provide financial support directly to people in poverty
- Engage nonprofit organizations, cooperatives, corporations, small businesses, self-help groups, and community-based organizations in assisting local communities to carry out a range of implementation activities, not just financial assistance
- Monitor, evaluate, and revise strategies and tactics (with detailed evaluations and strategic and tactical revisions every five years during the program)
- Sanction non-compliant countries, corporations, and high-income people (for example, with tariff restrictions)

7

Develop and implement a range of programs that promote and contribute to a positive sense of community in urban and rural places around the world

- Promoting sense of community can be woven into locally-oriented development programs all over the world. Examples include the rural community health initiative in Kenya that I mentioned above. What makes projects like this work is that they are based on local community members choosing priority health issues and acting on them together by selecting local residents to be trained as community health workers, by improving local sanitary practices, by developing clean water systems, by reducing mosquito habitats, etc. Local residents work together to carry out these activities, and, thus, strengthen their sense of community.

- Facilitators can be trained in techniques to improve sense of community by working with local residents to address a wide range of issues in addition to healthcare, including building local schools, organizing community solar projects, improving relationships between residents and police, and reducing gang violence and drug trafficking. Success on these kinds of projects has a simultaneous effect on community-building.

Conclusion

This chapter has emphasized the elimination of extreme poverty as a key condition for improving quality of life around the world. At the same time, it has stressed that "sense of community" is an important component of quality of life that is not easily measured compared to measuring the availability of basic goods and services.

The UN's Millennium Development Goals program was cited as a major success in improving quality of life around the world from 2000 to 2015. The Sustainable Development Goals program that followed the MDG program has not been as successful thus far but could be reinvigorated until it ends in 2030. A third program could be implemented from 2031 to 2050. The chapter concludes with seven sets of recommendations to increase the likelihood that everyone on the planet can have a decent quality of life by 2050.

One of the Sustainable Development Goals is to "take urgent action to combat climate change and its impacts."[345] This goal is the subject of the next chapter, and a major component in transitioning to an international cooperative economy.

Chapter 10

Creating a Sustainable Environment

Introduction

An era of extreme climate change

In a late July 2023 UN news report, Secretary General António Guterres is quoted as saying, "The era of global warming has ended" and "the era of global boiling has arrived."[346]

In mid-January, 2024, Dr. Sarah Kapnick, Chief Scientist of the US National Oceanic and Atmospheric Administration, stated that, "After seeing the 2023 climate analysis, I have to pause and say that the findings are astounding.… Not only was 2023 the warmest year in NOAA's 174-year climate record — it was the warmest by far."[347]

Some scientists reported that July 2023 was the warmest month for the earth's surface temperature in more than 100,000 years.[348]

Not only that, the high spring and early summer temperatures triggered a host of weather-related disasters. There were immense wildfires in multiple locations around the world. People living in the Midwest and Northeast United States were inundated by smoke from Canada's most severe wildfire season ever.[349] On a number of days, half or more of the U.S. population was cautioned by meteorologists not to go outside because of life-threatening heat and/or polluted air.[350] In July, the Greek island of Rhodes was evacuated because of out-of-control fires.[351] Well over 100 deaths resulted from torrential rains and flash floods in India and Sikkim in October.[352]

Fossil fuel industry leaders deny responsibility

In an early March 2024 article that was published in *The Guardian*,[353] Darren Woods, chief executive of ExxonMobil, the world's largest investor-owned oil company, asserted that "'The world is off track to meet its climate goals and the public is to blame.' Exxon is among the top contributors to global planet-heating greenhouse gas emissions. But Woods argued that big oil is not primarily responsible for the climate crisis."

As *The Guardian* article went on to report, "Experts say Woods's rhetoric is part of a larger attempt to skirt climate accountability. No new major oil and gas infrastructure can be built if the world is to avoid breaching agreed temperature limits, but Exxon, along with other major oil companies currently basking in record profits, is pushing ahead with aggressive fossil-fuel expansion plans. 'It's like a drug lord blaming everyone but himself for drug problems,' said Gernot Wagner, a climate economist at Columbia business school."

In a similar vein to Woods's comments, Amin H. Nasser, the CEO of Saudi Aramco, the world's largest oil and natural gas company, recently labeled the phaseout of fossil fuels as a "fantasy."[354]

The source of 80% of CO2 emissions

To underscore what the real fantasyland is, one needs only to look at *The Carbon Majors Database Launch Report* published in April 2024.[355] One of the most startling statistics in the report is that "57 fossil fuel and cement producers [are] linked to 80% of global fossil CO2 emissions since the Paris Agreement" signed by 196 Parties at the UN Climate Change Conference in 2015. In other words, the world's fossil fuel emissions could be radically reduced by changing the behavior of a few dozen companies.

RANKING OF GLOBAL CO2 EMISSIONS

1	China (Coal)	25.8%
2	Saudi Aramco	4.8%
3	Gazprom (Russia)	3.3%
4	Coal India	3.0%
5	National Iranian Oil Co.	2.8%
11	ExxonMobil	1.4%

Source: *Carbon Majors Data Launch Report,*[410] page 31

Note in the above table that China Coal alone accounts for more than a quarter of the world's carbon emissions. China increased coal production in 2023 by 2% over its 2022 production level. China's policy is to begin to reduce its coal production in 2025, and not achieve carbon neutrality until 2060.[356]

Why aren't we able to swiftly ameliorate the climate crisis?

The basic answer is that the world's economic problem-solving model is broken. We are deferring to those most responsible for global warming and other world problems – large for-profit corporations, powerful governments, and their enabling political and economic elites – to solve the very problems that they are responsible for creating and perpetuating. Wagner's reference to drug lords is a very apt analogy.

So, we need a new paradigm, one based on putting the well-being of the many ahead of the profits and power of the few.

Environmental sustainability

In the introduction to this book, environmental sustainability is defined as "meeting the needs of the present without compromising the ability of future generations to meet their own needs."[357] I also introduced the concept of human ecology as the "study of the relationship between humans and their natural, social, and built environments."[358]

As we know, the earth's environment is composed of land, water, air, and living organisms. All of these interconnected components need to be protected and nurtured in order to meet the goal of sustainability and to transition to a cooperative world economy during the 21st century.

This chapter focuses on the environmental threats posed by global warming. This is not to discount the importance of other environmental issues, but rather to give primary attention to the current problem that most affects the survival of our species and the world as we know it. Global warming threatens food production, adequate water resources, air quality, health, safe housing, and other components of sustainable development. It is also causing ecological changes that affect almost all life on earth at a rate far faster than most species' ability to adapt. This environmental instability is primarily a result of the accelerated burning of fossil fuels that began in the 1800s. Without an immediate, dramatic shift away from the use of coal, oil, and natural gas to solar, wind, and other clean energy sources, we are sentencing both ourselves and our descendants to a period of elevated temperatures and climate instability that could last for centuries.[359]

The remainder of the chapter presents information on our failure thus far to combat the climate crisis effectively, and then presents some recommendations on how countries, corporations, communities, and individuals can develop and implement a set of strategies and tactics that more effectively addresses the problems of global warming.

Recent trends in climate change policies and actions around the world

The world's slow response to addressing global warming

Global warming caused by the burning of fossil fuels was raised as a potential problem by the Swedish scientist Svante Arrhenius in 1896. It wasn't until the 1980s, however, that a significant segment of the scientific community began to sound the alarm about the imminent dangers posed by climate change.[360]

The alarm bells were eventually heard by the United Nations in 1992, which launched the first international initiative to address problems related to climate change at the "Earth Summit," held in Rio de Janeiro.[361] The UN Framework Convention on Climate Change that emerged from the summit "called for ongoing scientific research and regular meetings, negotiations, and future policy agreements designed to allow ecosystems to adapt naturally to climate change, to ensure that food production is not threatened, and to enable economic development to proceed in a sustainable manner."[362]

Since the Rio Summit, progress has been slow in turning this proclamation into concerted action. The Kyoto Protocol was adopted in December 1997, but didn't take effect until February 2005. There were 192 Parties to the Kyoto Protocol. However, it set modest, five-year emission-reduction targets for only the 37 most industrialized countries and the European Union.[363]

It wasn't until the Paris Agreement in December 2015 that UN members entered into a legally binding, but mushy (to be described later), international treaty on climate change. The agreement took effect in November 2016, with the goal of "a climate neutral world by mid-century."[364]

There were two primary related goals set in the Paris Agreement: "keeping a global temperature rise this century well below 2 degrees Celsius above pre-industrial levels, and to pursue efforts to limit the temperature increase even further to 1.5 degrees Celsius."[365]

In late November and early December 2023, the United Nations held a climate change conference in the United Arab Emirates. In UN jargon, the event was referred to as COP28, which stands for the 28th gathering of the Conference of the Parties. The conference now includes just about every country in the world and has been held almost every year since the UN Framework Convention on Climate Change was signed in Rio in 1992.

COP28 was a particularly important event because its primary tasks were to review progress made by governments on their emission reduction commitments – also known as Nationally Determined Contributions or NDCs – and to agree on next steps in reducing global warming.[366]

Most countries have done poorly in carrying out their fair share of the climate change goals set in Paris. This has been especially true for countries highly dependent on fossil fuel production. Because emission reduction commitments were "nationally determined" and, thus, voluntary, some countries set low reduction goals, or fell short of their own NDCs. Thus, my use of the word "mushy" above.

On our present course, we are very likely to exceed the 1.5°C threshold by some time in the early 2030s. As António Guterres, Secretary General of the United Nations, said to a group of world leaders in September 2022, the 1.5°C goal is "on life support." The problem is getting worse, not better. Mr. Guterres told the leaders that although emissions must be cut almost in half before 2030 to achieve the Paris Agreement goals, they are on track to rise by 14 percent. He added, "We are sleepwalking to climate catastrophe.[367]

The net effect of this poor performance as calculated by Climate Action Tracker in December 2023 was that the global temperature increase would reach 2.7°C by 2100 based on the current policies and actions of the world's governments.[368] This is well above the targets set in the Paris Agreement. One study reports that about two billion people or 20 percent of the world's population will be exposed to dangerous heat conditions if global warming reaches 2.7° Celsius by the end of the century.[369]

In summary, more than 30 years after the Summit in Rio, the world still has not gotten its act together to effectively address global warming.

The consequences of delayed action

There are major, negative economic consequences for failing to achieve rapid progress in reducing global warming. According to the *Global Turning Point Report*, published by Deloitte in May 2022, "Inaction on climate change could cost the world economy US$178 trillion by 2070. … By contrast the global economy could gain US$43 trillion over the next five decades by rapidly accelerating the transition to net-zero [greenhouse gas emissions]."[370]

The consequences of global warming are not just measured in dollars or other currencies. They are also measured by their impact on people's lives and on the environment. The longer we take to make the transition to clean energy sources – such as solar, wind, geothermal energy, hydropower, and other sources that don't emit carbon and other harmful gases – the more human suffering we will cause and the more damage we will inflict on the environment.[371]

The key components of a transition to a clean energy economy

Put simply, solving the problem of global warming will require a complete phaseout of fossil fuel use, accompanied by a rapid transition to a 100% renewable energy economy.

This is much easier said than done. The primary obstacle is the refusal, thus far, of most major fossil fuel production and distribution companies, their financiers and insurers, and the countries in which they are located to commit to such a phaseout. This was clearly evident at the COP28 Summit in Dubai, presided over by the CEO of the United Arab Emirates state-owned oil company.[372]

A report commissioned by the International Institute for Sustainable Development and published in March 2023 drew the following conclusion: "To comply with the carbon budget for a 50:50 chance of not exceeding 1.5°C of warming requires immediate and deep cuts in the production of all fossil fuels. There are no exceptions; all nations need to begin a rapid and just phase-out of existing production. The report makes absolutely clear that there is no capacity in the carbon budget for opening up new production facilities of any kind, whether coal mines, oil wells or gas terminals. A transition based on principles of equity requires wealthy, high-emitting nations to phase out all oil and gas production by 2034 while the poorest nations have until 2050 to end production." [373]

But there is nothing to indicate that such a transition is about to happen. In fact, as a recent report from Climate Action Tracker indicates, fossil fuel consumption (and thus global warming) is projected to continue to increase rather than decrease well beyond 2030. [374]

Note also that getting past peak fossil fuel consumption is only a prelude to declining emissions. The National Oceanic and Atmospheric Administration published an article in October 2022 states that, "If all human emissions of heat-trapping gases were to stop today, Earth's temperature would continue to rise for a few decades as ocean currents bring excess heat stored in the deep ocean back to the surface. Once this excess heat radiated out to space, Earth's temperature would stabilize. Experts think the additional warming from this "hidden" heat is unlikely to exceed 0.9° Fahrenheit (0.5°Celsius). With no further human influence, natural processes would begin to slowly remove the excess carbon dioxide from the atmosphere, and global temperatures would gradually begin to decline. [375]

However, "human emissions of heat-trapping gases" are not going to stop today. They are likely to continue into the second half of the 21st century and cause increasing catastrophic events in the remainder of this century and beyond.

Recommendations for effective climate change action in the next quarter century

This section of the chapter contains several recommendations on how the world can get beyond its ineffective, and often counterproductive, actions in slowing, and eventually reducing, global warming.

Reducing the market for fossil fuels

In early December 2023, most of the countries of the world wrangled with Saudi Arabia and other petrostates and fossil fuel companies at COP28 – the recent climate change conference in Dubai – over whether there should be an explicit reference to a phaseout of fossil fuels in the conference's final agreement. The debate went far into overtime, and the pro-phaseout advocates appeared to have won the battle.[376] However, a closer look at that agreement shows that the victory is illusory. It's a non-binding agreement with a plethora of options that "Dirty Energy" can use to subvert it. The language in the agreement does not explicitly call for a phaseout of fossil fuels, but rather for a "transitioning away from fossil fuels.… so as to achieve net zero by 2050…"[377] One could write a book solely on the ambiguity of the words "transitioning away from."

Despite the many loopholes, there is hope for a genuine phaseout of the vast majority of fossil fuels by 2050. It won't happen by trusting the goodwill of the fossil fuel-producing companies and their allies but, instead, by reducing the demand for these fuels as quickly as possible.

How do we reduce demand?

The short answer is by continuing to reduce the relative cost of clean energy compared to dirty energy. We need to accelerate the deployment of clean energy in both the Global North and the Global South, rapidly increase energy efficiency, make trillions of dollars available for the expansion of clean energy resources, provide support to energy-poor and vulnerable countries to cope with the harmful effects of climate change, and end subsidies to the producers and distributors of dirty fuels.

Basic economics tells us that no matter how much fossil fuel companies can produce, they won't be able to sell their products if they are not competitive in the marketplace. In other words, dirty energy companies can control the supply of their products, but they can't control demand for them. As demand dries up, the market for oil, gas, and coal will disappear.

Examples

Let's dig a little deeper into this demand-side strategy for phasing out dirty energy. The best place to start is with a couple of good examples. In 2023, the European Union enacted "Fit for 55"[378] as a package of programs to accelerate the EU's reduction of carbon emissions – with the goals of achieving a 55% reduction of emissions in 2030 compared to those in 1990, and net zero carbon emissions by 2050. The main components of Fit for 55 are:

- An emissions trading system (ETS) that gradually increases the cost of carbon emissions by both domestic "operators" and by companies wanting to export goods to EU member countries

- The addition of several new target emitters to those already subject to the ETS, including shipping, aviation, road transport, and energy-inefficient buildings

- Clear, measurable goals and increasingly severe consequences for operators failing to meet the goals that are built into the system

- Periodic updating of the implementation strategy based on changing conditions

- A carbon border adjustment mechanism that effectively imposes carbon taxes on companies operating outside the EU that market their products to the EU. These carbon taxes protect EU-based companies from unfair competition.

In summary, this strategy is a straightforward, clearly understandable means to reduce fossil fuel use and greenhouse gas emissions in order to achieve the 2030 and 2050 Paris Agreement goals.

Note that there are flaws in the Fit for 55 strategy. For example, Climate Action Tracker, reported in February 2024 that "The EU is not yet on track to meet its 2030 target to reduce emissions by at least 55% below 1990. ... Having the legislative framework in place to meet its 2030 NDC target is an important step, but rapid implementation of policies and measures at member state level is crucial for it to become a reality."[379] The report also criticized the EU strategy for "fail[ing] to contribute its fair share to global climate action, and should. ... substantially increase its climate finance support to countries in the Global South."[380]

Thirteen states in the United States provide another set of examples of demand-side programs to reduce fossil fuel use.[381] Like the European Union, these states also use carbon-pricing mechanisms to ratchet down fossil fuel use by utilities and other companies. What makes this a big deal is that these states have a significant presence in the world economy. If California were a country, it would have the fifth largest economy in the world.

Expanding the EU's and United States' initiatives

The world needs a Carbon Reduction Initiative II – a broad, international coalition of countries that would accelerate their pace of change toward an increased use of clean energy. If the United States, the United Kingdom, Australia, Japan, South Korea, and dozens of other countries were to enact carbon taxes on domestically produced and imported goods, China, India, Russia, and other major oil-, gas-, and coal-producing states and companies would be far more inclined to abandon their dirty energy ways.

There are a range of other components to this demand-side strategy favoring clean energy over dirty energy. Clean energy is less expensive (and on course to being even more economical in the decades ahead). It's also a far less risky long-term investment for companies and countries that are likely to face stranded assets when the value of their fossil fuel energy reserves decreases as demand drops off. The longer these countries and companies wait to join the clean energy bandwagon, the more expensive their energy transitions will be.

Clean energy also doesn't pose the health risks of fossil fuels such as polluted communities; accidents arising from production, distribution, and industrial applications; and environmentally ravaged landscapes.

Legal challenges against fossil fuel companies are also on the rise within countries and in international courts. These costly challenges are based on the environmental degradation, overvaluation, and lies that fossil fuel companies have spread about the "benefits" of their products.

Expanded financing for addressing climate change problems in the Global South

The demand-side approach could be enlarged dramatically in the next few years, especially if funds were available to developing countries to accelerate their clean energy growth.[382]

In April 2024, two different financial strategies were proposed to assist countries in the Global South to respond to climate change problems. One would be based on a carbon tax on fossil fuel companies headquartered in OECD countries beginning in 2024. If the tax had "an initial rate of $5 a tonne [a little over 2200 pounds] of CO2 equivalent, increasing by $5 a tonne each year, it would raise a total of $900bn by 2030."[383]

The other financial approach would be based on "a low-interest World Bank facility for developing nations that they [would] rely on to help fund their development and combat climate change. Donors will make their cash pledges to the International Development Association (IDA), a World Bank institution that offers loans with low interest rates and long tenures." The goal of the initiative would be to increase[e] IDA contributions…to at least $120 billion.[384]

As reported in a UN press release, "The United Nations Climate Change conference, COP28, has concluded with a historic agreement to transition away from fossil fuels, triple renewable energy and increase climate finance for the most vulnerable."[385]

We have the potential to make this agreement more than just a set of vague, easily broken promises, especially through concerted efforts to increase the use of clean energy and to rapidly reduce demand for fossil fuels. This demand-side strategy can make a dramatic difference by 2030 despite the disingenuous actions of Dirty Energy to continue the world's dependency on fossil fuels for as long as possible.

Conclusion

It's way past time to get serious about the war on global warming. Our current economic paradigm isn't working. We need to figure out a revised strategy for success. The European Union is beginning to show the rest of the world by example how to reduce and eventually eliminate the demand for fossil fuels.

The next chapter presents four scenarios for what the world's economies might look like in 2050. How well – or poorly – we address the problem of global warming figures prominently into all four alternatives.

Chapter 11

Four Scenarios
for the World Economy in 2050

Introduction

Predictions are a tricky business. In this chapter, I will hedge my bets by forecasting four alternative world economies in 2050 – what I refer to as ugly, bad, mediocre, and cooperative scenarios. As the reader may expect, I will give most attention to the cooperative option, which will also be the subject of the next chapter.

Clearly there are more than four ways the future could play out during the next quarter century. In order to avoid predictions that are too broad and sketchy, this chapter will be based on an integrated synopsis of the information and recommendations presented in the previous chapters of the book. I focus on the strengths and weaknesses of our current economic system; the seeds of change emerging in this system; the impact of cooperatives and civil society organizations and legislative protections in reducing greed and uncertainty in the world's mixed economies; and the status of political and economic democracy, quality of life, and the sustainability of the environment.

An ugly economy in 2050

An increase in the world temperature by 2050 that significantly exceeds the Paris Agreement goal of 2° Celsius (3.6° Fahrenheit) would be the main factor shaping an ugly economy.

A 2021 report published by the International Panel on Climate Change (IPCC) calculated that "With every additional increment of global warming, changes in extremes continue to become larger.

For example, every additional 0.5°C of global warming causes clearly discernible increases in the intensity and frequency of hot extremes, including heatwaves. … and heavy precipitation. … as well as agricultural and ecological droughts."[386]

Several projections by climate scientists indicate that the world's temperature may reach 3°C this century, possibly even as early as 2050.[387] [388] Daniel Swain of the University of California, Los Angeles, commented that such a temperature increase would be, "Bad for humans. Bad for ecosystems. Bad for the stability of the Earth systems that we humans depend on for everything."[389]

According to a recent article in BuzzFeedNews, "In such a brutally hot world, scientists agree, deadly heat waves, massive wildfires, and damaging downpours will come far more often and hit much harder than they do today. The ocean will be hotter too and more acidic, causing fish declines and likely the end of coral reefs. In fact, a quarter or so of the Earth's species may go extinct in such conditions or be headed that way. Our coastlines would be reshaped, a consequence of sea levels rising foot after foot, century after century, drowning places like Charleston, South Carolina's Market Street, downtown Providence, Rhode Island, and the Space Center in Houston."[390]

An increase of 3°C (5.4°F) or more by 2050 would not only have strong impacts on weather-related events around the world, it would also have serious negative consequences for both democracy and quality of life. Increasingly high temperatures – along with severe droughts and floods – would trigger major health problems, provoke an increase in domestic and international conflicts, and cause unprecedented migration as hundreds of millions of people would seek to relocate away from the most inhospitable regions.[391]

It's hard to imagine democracy holding its own or people around the world having a decent quality of life in such a chaotic physical world.

A bad economy in 2050

The bad economy projected here is a continuation of the generally poor current international patterns and trends in democracy, quality of life, and the climate in the early 2020s.

Political democracy

One characteristic of democracy in a bad economy would be that less than half – between 40% and 50% – of the world's population is living in democratic countries by mid-century. This scenario is based on the assumption that the gradual slide in democracy in the early 21st century would continue or, at best, level off during the second quarter of the century. As the most populous country, India alone could tip the balance to a primarily hybrid and authoritarian world if it continues on its present trend of depriving non-Hindus of their political rights.

Economic democracy

Labor, consumer, and other civil society rights correlate closely with political democracy. Thus, a stagnant or declining trend in the latter is likely to have a stifling impact on these rights. It is more difficult to project the impact of political stagnation on the future of cooperatives. If the international cooperative movement were to improve its level of involvement and coordination in cooperative development, there could even be an increase in the number of well-functioning cooperatives by 2050 under this scenario, despite an overall bad economy.

Quality of life

Barring a dramatic increase in the world's temperature, the bad economic scenario projects an average quality of life around the world that would be slightly worse than, or about the same as, that in the early 2020s. This projection is in line with the recent lack of progress in achieving the United Nations' Sustainable Development Goals, discussed in chapter 9.

Environmental sustainability

The bad scenario is based on some progress in fighting global warming during the next quarter century – enough to keep us from blowing too far past the 2°C goal. Since 2010, there have been encouraging developments in the areas of renewable energy and energy efficiency.[392] [393] On the other hand, fossil fuel production and consumption have also been increasing during this same time period.[394]

A mediocre economy in 2050

A mediocre economy would see a moderate improvement in democracy and quality of life by 2050. The rise in greenhouse gas emissions and the accompanying increase in the world temperature would continue, but at a slower pace than projected in the ugly and bad scenarios.

Political democracy

The mediocre scenario assumes that the coalition of democratic countries that supported Ukraine after it was invaded by Russia would continue after the war. It also assumes a gradual improvement in democracy in other countries, bringing the percentage of people living in democracies above 50%.

Economic democracy

Since both the level of civil society rights and the number of cooperative enterprises correlate with political democracy, there's a good chance for these economic democracy components to increase slightly in a mediocre economy.

Quality of life

With the Russia-Ukraine war and the COVID pandemic over, the member countries of the United Nations would be able to salvage some progress in the Sustainable Development Goals program by 2030, and would initiate another round of quality-of-life improvements between 2031 and 2050. Thus, there would likely be a decrease in extreme poverty, an increase in access to healthcare, and a minor-to-moderate improvement in quality of life around the world.

Environmental sustainability

Like the bad economy model, the mediocre economy scenario assumes a moderate increase in greenhouse gas emissions and the beginning of a long, gradual bending of the curve toward a lower global temperature by 2050.

A cooperative economy in 2050

A cooperative economy would be characterized by a substantial improvement in political and economic democracy and quality of life around the world. We would be at or close to net zero greenhouse gas emissions for the first time since the early years of the industrial revolution.

Political democracy

As discussed in chapter 8, a variety of paths lead to democracy. Domestic pro-democracy and anti-corruption movements have the potential to increase the number of democratic countries. Unlike the failed efforts of the Arab Spring pro-democracy protests of the early 2010s, future movements have the potential to be tied more closely to political parties, electoral politics, and constitutional reforms and, therefore, to have a greater likelihood of institutionalizing political reform.

Support by the international community could also help promote democracy by providing development aid to countries, cooperatives, and for-profit and nonprofit organizations. This aid would include strict auditing requirements, performance monitoring, and enforced consequences for misuse of aid project funding.

Economic democracy

Again, the correlation between political and economic democracy bodes well for improved labor, consumer, and other civil society rights, and for an atmosphere in which cooperative enterprises could flourish.

Quality of life

The successful implementation of the UN's Millennium Development Goals program from 2000 to 2015 provides strong evidence that concerted efforts can make dramatic improvements in quality of life. A recommitment to the Sustainable Development Goals program in 2024 through 2030, and a follow-up program from 2031 through 2050, could support a considerable improvement in quality of life around the world.

Environmental sustainability

The cooperative economic scenario assumes that we would be at or near zero greenhouse gas emissions by 2050. However, given that carbon and other harmful gas emissions have a prolonged impact on global temperature, climate-related disasters would continue to rise and not begin to taper off until the end of the 21st century or later.

In the mid-2020s, we are still primarily dependent on fossil fuels for our energy needs, despite major improvements in renewable energy and energy conservation. Many countries, corporations, and individuals are not yet committed to the war on global warming. Some companies and countries, in fact, are hiding behind "green-washed" pronouncements that effectively provide cover for increasing greenhouse gas emissions. So, carbon emission reduction strategies similar to those of the European Union, including carefully developed and monitored incentives and enforced sanctions, would be required to reach net zero emissions by 2050.

Conclusion

We have all the ingredients to create a prosperous, peaceful world society. What's missing is the will to do so and a set of strategies that combine these ingredients into the early stages of a cooperative world economy by 2050. The next chapter focuses on how we might begin a systematic transition to a cooperative world economy in the next quarter century.

Transitioning to a More Cooperative World Economy

Introduction

The Industrial Revolution began only about 250 years ago, and the rate of economic and technological change has increased exponentially since then. Thus, projecting dramatic economic, political, social, and environmental change during the next quarter of a century is not at all far-fetched.

Our descendants could very well look back from 2100 to the second quarter of this century and react with disgust at the political and economic disarray, the extreme inequality, and the environmental irresponsibility of their forebears. Or they could look back with gratitude at the innovations we instituted to increase democratic governance, reduce economic inequality, and begin the long process of healing the world's environment.

This chapter is intended to summarize the changes required in our economic behavior so that our grandchildren and great grandchildren view us with gratitude rather than disgust.

The cooperative economy is a process rather than an endpoint

The world, and our place in it, will always be in flux. We can set goals for improving our positive role in the world. And we can make course corrections from time to time without losing sight of our long-term commitment to a world society and economy that empowers people, improves the quality of our lives, and works to restore the damage we have done to our environment.

We have all of the makings for this kind of constructive relationship among ourselves and with nature during the next quarter of a century. The big issue is whether we have the will to begin a new economic paradigm and coordinate these activities in a short period of time at local, regional, national, and international levels.

As I have maintained in the latter half of the book, the seeds of a cooperative world economy are already sprouting. The following story about Sweden exemplifies this transition.

The example of Sweden

Sweden wasn't always the peaceful, prosperous, and democratic country that it is today. The Vikings from what is now Sweden, Denmark, and Norway raided and pillaged their way through Europe from the late 8th to the late 11th centuries. Sweden lost about a third of its population to a bubonic plague in the 14th century. By the 17th century, Sweden had become the third-largest country in Europe, measured by land mass, and then ceded most of its territory to other countries in the early 18th century. Its population doubled between 1750 and 1850, precipitating a wave of emigration in response to famine and rebellion. By 1910, more than one million Swedes had emigrated to the United States alone.[395]

Sweden became a parliamentary democracy in the early 20th century.[396] It is currently ranked as one of the most democratic countries in the world.[397] With a population of about 10.4 million, the country has developed a successful model of a democratic mixed economy. In 2022, Sweden's gross domestic product per capita was 23rd among major economies.[398] More than 10% of the country's GDP is provided by cooperatives, and Sweden has a strong labor union movement.[399] Its welfare system, including universal healthcare, free education through the college level, and a generous social security program, is considered to be among the best in the world.[400] Sweden is

*also among the world's leaders in countering climate change,
including a commitment to achieve net-zero carbon emissions by 2045. Its citizens have a mixed record on supporting
immigration.*

Goals for improving the world economy by 2050

In the previous chapter, I presented four scenarios for what the
world economy could look like in the next quarter century. Three
of them are severely to moderately grim. In this chapter, I make
the case that there is good potential for the non-grim option – a
more cooperative world economy.

To make this case, I focus on those countries and regions of the
world that are already showing signs of developing more cooperative economies. Then, I look at other countries and regions and an-
alyze how a substantial number of them could join this transition.

Similar to the case study of Sweden above, I evaluate the political democracy, economic democracy, quality of life, and environmental sustainability of several regions and countries. I also
attempt to chart realistic paths from where these economies are to
a more cooperative economic future. Then I step back and make a
preliminary determination of how the world economy as a whole
might become more cooperative by 2050.

My goal all along in this book has been to use measurable objectives to determine whether we are moving closer to a cooperative world economy. Thus, it would be theoretically possible to
carry out a quantitative analysis of this question. However, the
measurement tools and longitudinal data for such an analysis on
a world scale just aren't there yet. In the meantime, I will need to
take a less rigorous approach.

The remainder of the chapter focuses on the main changes necessary to put the world on track to becoming a more cooperative economy by 2050. It reviews the major issues that need to be

addressed relative to the four components of a cooperative world economy analyzed in this book – political democracy, economic democracy, quality of life, and environmental sustainability.

The book has had 11 chapters of build-up – starting with chimpanzee economies; reviewing the characteristics and spread of modern human hunting and gathering economies dating back 300,000 years; summarizing our transition to agricultural economies beginning about 12,000 years ago; tracking the emergence of villages, cities, city states, and empires – and the wars and trade relationships among them – during the past 5,000 years; witnessing the end of most of these empires in the first half of the 20th century; and observing the emergence of a world of about 200 nations with a wide range of very unequal, mixed economies in the latter half of the 20th century and the first quarter of the 21st century.

We evaluated the strengths and weaknesses of our current set of mixed economies and the relationships among them, coming away with an awareness of major problems related to political and economic democracy, dramatically unequal quality of life for people around the world, and the threat of global warming representing the largest human-made crisis the world has ever faced. This is the chapter that gets us to the dénouement: How can we make meaningful progress toward creating a worldwide cooperative economy by 2050?

The key phrase above, "meaningful progress," requires a bit more specificity.

For political democracy, the goal is that most of the world's population will be living in full or flawed democratic countries by 2050.

The goals for economic democracy and quality of life are not as clearly defined. In the case of economic democracy, I use a two-part measure: 1) growth in the number of well-functioning cooperatives and an increase in the number of cooperative members; and 2) improvements in the control of workers, consumers, local community residents, and small business owners over their lives. These are not simple factors to measure but are nonetheless essential aspects of a more cooperative economy.

An increased sense of community experienced by people around the world is a somewhat nebulous, but important, goal for improved quality of life. I couple this amorphous goal with a range of improvements related to reducing poverty and hunger and improving our health and other aspects of our physical well-being. Many of these goals are well represented in the United Nations' development goals programs, so I refer to the UN development goals as a means to evaluate the extent to which we are improving our quality of life as we approach 2050.

Environmental sustainability is a broad concept encompassing the relationships between humans and the environments in which we live. Because of the existential crisis precipitated by human-made warming of the world's temperature – and the consequent disasters that this has caused and will continue to cause at increasingly severe levels – I use substantially reducing the amount of carbon dioxide and other greenhouse gas emissions by 2050 as the primary measure of environmental sustainability. This measure is based on how close we come to the Paris Accord's goal of keeping the world's temperature below 2°C above preindustrial levels by 2050.

So, the decisive question is: Can we achieve meaningful progress on these goals by 2050?

This section of the chapter makes the case that we can, even though we are currently well off-track from doing so. The section provides an overview of the barriers to, and opportunities for, making meaningful progress toward a more cooperative world economy by 2050.

Political democracy

About 45% of the world's population was living in democracies at the end of 2023.[401] How can we bring that percentage above 50% by 2050?

Threats to democracy as perceived in early 2024:

- The election of anti-democratic leaders in previously democratic countries, for example, Trump's possible re-election as president of the United States
- Putin's invasion of Ukraine and Russia's threat to the NATO alliance
- China's abysmal human rights record at home and saber-rattling abroad, especially regarding Taiwan
- Hindu populism in India
- The war between Hamas and Israel and the political instability in the Middle East
- Right-wing extremism in Europe and Latin America
- The weakening of democracy in some Sub-Saharan African countries
- International terrorism

Opportunities for increasing political democracy

As I have contended in other parts of the book, stable, political democracies are a necessary condition for secure, long-term progress on all the components of a cooperative economy.

Oligarchies and autocracies are inherently prone to be periodically overthrown, and with their demise, their policies – good and bad – are usually tossed out as well. Well-structured political democracies change their leaders through free and fair elections held on a regular, peaceful basis every few years. Thus, these countries are far more likely to maintain supportive policies related to economic democracy, quality of life, and environmental sustainability over the long term and not have these policies dramatically disrupted by abrupt changes in political leadership at the top.

Countries with high per capita incomes tend to be full or flawed democracies.[402] The major exception to this pattern is wealthy authoritarian petrostates, which derive the predominant part of their national incomes from export sales of oil and natural gas. Especially in the Middle East, these countries have a large percentage of "guest" workers. Thus, the citizenry is small and generally well-off economically. This is likely to change in the near future as the demand for oil and gas decreases due to the threat of global warming.[403]

In general, as countries become better off in terms of longevity and health, level of education, income levels, and other quality-of-life characteristics, they are more likely to be or become political democracies. Thus, a major part of the strategy of increasing political democracy and moving toward a more cooperative economy by 2050 is to promote and assist in the development of these positive social, health, and economic traits.

There are 34 hybrid regimes in the world that lie somewhere between democratic and authoritarian.[404] They include some of the largest countries in the world, such as Nigeria, Bangladesh, Mexico, and Pakistan. A renewed emphasis on funding and implementing the UN development goals appears to be an excellent means to turn some of these hybrid countries into democracies and thus increase the number of people living in democracies in the world.

Similarly, progress toward phasing out fossil fuels and reducing carbon emissions (which is also one of the UN sustainable development goals) would improve the quality of life of billions of people and, thus, increase the number of people living in democracies by 2050.

Economic democracy

Potential increases in the number of cooperatives and the strengthening of labor, consumer, and other civil society organizations, along with legal protections for these organizations, also have good potential to move the world toward a more cooperative economy by 2050.

As discussed in chapter 7, economic democracy is an important measure of the extent to which a country is considered to have a cooperative economy. However, the scientific literature on economic democracy does not provide an agreed-upon definition, and a consistent measure of economic democracy has not yet been developed and used on an international level. Thus, until such an agreed-upon definition and measurement system have been developed, I'm using a provisional approach in this book, which is based on two primary considerations: 1) the extent to which a national economy is made up of cooperative enterprises; 2) the protection and expansion of labor, consumer, and other civil society organizations.

Threats to economic democracy in the next quarter century

The biggest threats to economic democracy between now and 2050 are primarily the same threats faced by political democracy. If most people around the world are not living in political democracies, there is very little likelihood that they will have access to democratically controlled businesses or meaningful participation in labor, consumer, and other civil society organizations.

Opportunities for increasing economic democracy

Improved coordination among cooperative development organizations, especially in the Global South, would be a key factor in accelerating the rate of formation, evaluation, and improved functioning of cooperatives by 2050.[405]

Of particular note is that the General Assembly of the United Nations recently designated 2025 as the International Year of Cooperatives. This is the second time in the 21st century that the United Nations has recognized the importance of co-ops with such a designation.[406]

The United Nations also has the potential to play a lead role in strengthening civil society organizations around the world – both through a reinvigoration of the Sustainable Development Goals program that ends in 2030 and through the creation of a follow-on program, perhaps lasting from 2031 until 2050. In addition, the UN's International Labor Organization can play an ongoing role in promoting and protecting the rights of workers around the world.[407]

Following are my top priorities for increasing economic democracy in the world in the next quarter century:

- Leverage the UN designation establishing 2025 as the International Year of Cooperatives by strengthening and expanding international co-op development institutions and programs. The most important set of actions that the international cooperative community can carry out in the decades ahead is to better coordinate international organizations, networks, and activities related to developing and strengthening cooperatives. The importance of better coordination is especially true in the Global South, where the need for cooperative development is the greatest – for example, in accomplishing the UN Sustainable Development Goals.

- There are similar opportunities for improving coordination among labor, consumer, and other economic democracy-related organizations. For example, The International Labor Organization of the United Nations is an excellent resource for strengthening regulations and laws related to the treatment of workforces around the world. The UN should play a similar role in protecting and expanding consumer and other civil society organizations.

Quality of life

Although difficult to implement and measure, successful initiatives to improve people's sense of community have the potential to increase within and among countries by 2050. As mentioned in chapter 9, there has been quite a bit of promising experimentation in community-building during the past several decades.

A recommitment to the UN's Sustainable Development Goals program and a new UN development goals program from 2031 to 2050 would also dramatically improve quality of life around the world.

Wealth and income inequality may very well decrease substantially by 2050 primarily due to reforms in domestic and international taxation systems and wealth-distribution programs.

A portion of the funds available for grants and sustainable investment resulting from a decrease in financial inequality may be used to improve the quality of life of low-income and low-wealth households around the world.

Environmental sustainability

There was a half-hearted, legalistic agreement by COP28 participants to transition away from fossil fuels at their December 2023 meeting. With the exception of petrostates and those highly dependent on coal-based economies, a majority of the world's countries appear to have a genuine commitment to a near-term fossil fuel phaseout in the 2020s and 2030s.[408]

The Fit for 55 program already being implemented by the European Union provides a partial template for such a phaseout. Fit for 55 is based on an emissions trading system that gradually increases the cost of carbon emissions by both domestic "operators" and by companies wanting to export goods to EU member countries. The program has clearly articulated, measurable goals, with increasingly severe consequences over time for operators failing to meet these goals. Moreover, periodic updating of the strategy based on changing conditions is built into the program administration. Finally, a carbon border adjustment mechanism is being put in place that will effectively tax companies exporting goods to the EU, preventing them from undercutting companies within the EU that are required to meet emission-reduction targets. Under the Fit for 55 program and other policies, the EU is on track to achieve net zero carbon emissions by 2050.

The EU strategy can be an effective model for other countries and regions because it ratchets down the demand for fossil fuels. It does this by making renewable energy sources and energy conservation less expensive alternatives to fossil fuels. This demand-driven approach is an effective way to counter the supply-based production strategies of fossil fuel countries and companies.

Weaving the four components into a more cooperative world economy

I discussed the concept of "demographic transition" in chapter 9 to provide a partial explanation for the decreasing birthrates associated with the increased social and economic security of women and couples in different countries and regions. These decreased birthrates are leading to a declining world population sometime in the latter part of the 21st century and will help to reduce the negative environmental footprint of our species on the planet.

One can posit a similar phenomenon – an "economic transition" – that could also occur in this century. As I have discussed in various parts of the book, the roots of the word "economy" are management and household – with household referring both to specific households and communities and to the world in which we live.

As our quality of life and sense of economic security increase, we have the potential to increase our involvement in actively shaping our social, political, and physical environments and to reduce the power of large for-profit corporations, extremely wealthy and powerful individuals, and the governments that enable their domination of the world economy. This shift in our economic paradigm may provide momentum for establishing increasingly cooperative economies at local, national, and international levels.

Conclusion

There is no guarantee that our species will make major progress in creating a more cooperative world economy by 2050. But as this chapter has shown, we have the capability to do so – especially if we interweave paradigm-changing reforms that increase our levels of political and economic democracy, improve the quality of life at all levels of society, and decrease carbon emissions.

What sets us apart as a species is our ability to plan and execute activities that can change the world. Especially during the past couple of centuries, we have abused this ability at a global level through conflict with one another and destruction of our environment. However, we are also capable of taking dramatic, positive action now and in the future.

Our ability to take such positive action is the major theme of this book and our best hope for creating a more cooperative world economy – with all of its corresponding benefits – in the next quarter century.

Conclusion

So, will our children and grandchildren look back at us from the second half of the 21st-century with gratitude or disgust?

The answer to that question largely depends on what we do to improve human behavior and our relationship with the environment during the next 25 years.

One thing that is reassuring is that *Homo sapiens* (Latin for "wise man") has survived as a species for about 300,000 years, successfully adapting to many changes along the way. The same cannot be said about our 20 or so sets of human cousins who are now extinct.

On the other hand, despite our adaptability so far, we may be on the verge of self-induced extinction, or, if not extinction, a significant worsening of our quality of life and physical environment.

Perhaps there is some kind of cosmic joke in this. We are the last humans standing, and then we do ourselves in.

One could easily question whether, in fact, our species is "wise." Other adjectives that may be as appropriate are greedy, self-centered, power-hungry, disrespectful toward one another and our environment, and a host of other pejorative terms.

But are these negative attributes our defining characteristics?

When I evaluate our pluses and minuses, I conclude that modern humans are a mix of divergent characteristics, some that exacerbate our conflicts with one another and with our environment, and others that foster cooperation and compatibility with nature.

As I implied at the end of chapter 12, our near-term future is not preordained by our inherent positive or negative traits as human beings, but rather will be determined by the actions we take – or fail to take – as a species.

Appendix:
Cooperative identity, values, and principles

This appendix is copied verbatim from the website of the International Cooperative Alliance.[409]

The International Cooperative Alliance is the global steward of the Statement on the Cooperative Identity – the Values and Principles of the cooperative movement.

In 1995, the ICA adopted the revised Statement on the Cooperative Identity which contains the definition of a cooperative, the values of cooperatives, and the seven cooperative principles as described below.

Definition of a Cooperative

A cooperative is an autonomous association of persons united voluntarily to meet their common economic, social and cultural needs and aspirations through a jointly-owned and democratically-controlled enterprise.

Cooperative Values

Cooperatives are based on the values of self-help, self-responsibility, democracy, equality, equity, and solidarity. In the tradition of their founders, cooperative members believe in the ethical values of honesty, openness, social responsibility and caring for others.

Cooperative Principles

The cooperative principles are guidelines by which cooperatives put their values into practice.

1. Voluntary and Open Membership

Cooperatives are voluntary organisations, open to all persons able to use their services and willing to accept the responsibilities of membership, without gender, social, racial, political or religious discrimination.

2. Democratic Member Control

Cooperatives are democratic organisations controlled by their members, who actively participate in setting their policies and making decisions. Men and women serving as elected representatives are accountable to the membership. In primary cooperatives members have equal voting rights (one member, one vote) and cooperatives at other levels are also organised in a democratic manner.

3. Member Economic Participation

Members contribute equitably to, and democratically control, the capital of their cooperative. At least part of that capital is usually the common property of the cooperative. Members usually receive limited compensation, if any, on capital subscribed as a condition of membership. Members allocate surpluses for any or all of the following purposes: developing their cooperative, possibly by setting up reserves, part of which at least would be indivisible; benefiting members in proportion to their transactions with the cooperative; and supporting other activities approved by the membership.

4. Autonomy and Independence

Cooperatives are autonomous, self-help organisations controlled by their members. If they enter into agreements with other organisations, including governments, or raise capital from external sources, they do so on terms that ensure democratic control by their members and maintain their cooperative autonomy.

5. Education, Training, and Information

Cooperatives provide education and training for their members, elected representatives, managers, and employees so they can contribute effectively to the development of their co-operatives. They inform the general public - particularly young people and opinion leaders - about the nature and benefits of co-operation.

6. Cooperation Among Cooperatives

Cooperatives serve their members most effectively and strengthen the cooperative movement by working together through local, national, regional and international structures.

7. Concern for Community

Cooperatives work for the sustainable development of their communities through policies approved by their members.

Endnotes

The following endnotes provide citations for information presented in the book. Note that I do not intend these citations to be overly academic. My intent is that they be easily accessible, useful references for readers who are interested in sources of information and, perhaps, in following up with more detailed research on topics of particular interest to them.

1. For example: Mills, C. Wright, *The Sociological Imagination,* Oxford University Press, 1959

2. Bush, Larry, "The Morphology of a Humorous Phrase: 'We have met the enemy and he is us,'" Humor in America, 2014, https://humorinamerica. wordpress.com/2014/05/19/the-morphology-of-a-humorous-phrase/

3. Nadeau, E.G., *The Cooperative Solution: How the United States can tame recessions, reduce inequality, and protect the environment,* The Cooperative Society Project, 2012, https://thecooperativesociety.org/ book-the-cooperative-solution/

4. "UN resolution calls for a second International Year of Cooperatives in 2025," International Cooperative Alliance, November 14, 2023, https://ica.coop/en/newsroom/news/ resolution-calls-second-international-year-cooperatives-2025

5. I use modern humans and *Homo sapiens* interchangeably in the book.

6. See for example: Barras, Colin, "Who are you? How the story of human origins is being rewritten," *New Scientist,* August 23, 2017, https://www. newscientist.com/article/mg23531400-500-who-are-you-how-the-story-of-human-origins-is-being-rewritten/

7.	"Economy," Wikipedia, accessed August 22, 2023, https://en.wikipedia.org/wiki/Economy

8.	"Democracy," Wikipedia, accessed August 22, 2023, https://en.wikipedia.org/wiki/Democracy#:~:text=Democracy%20(from%20Ancient%20Greek%3A%20δημοκρατία,(%22representative%20democracy%22)

9.	"Economic democracy," Wikipedia, accessed March 14, 2024, https://en.wikipedia.org/wiki/Economic_democracy

10.	Dubb, Steve, Ted Howard and Sarah McKinley, "Economic Democracy," in *Achieving Sustainability: Visions, Principles and Practices*, Debra Rowe, editor, Gale, 2014, pp. 231-239

11.	"What is a cooperative?" International Cooperative Alliance, accessed August 23, 2023, https://www.ica.coop/en/cooperatives/what-is-a-cooperative

12.	"Quality of Life Indicators," Federal Statistical Office, Section Environment, Sustainable Development, Territory, Espace de l'Europe 10, CH-2010 Neuchâtel, accessed August 23, 2023, Switzerland, https://www.bfs.admin.ch/bfs/en/home/statistics/cross-sectional-topics/city-statistics/indicators-quality-life.html

13.	"Civic engagement," Wikipedia, accessed March 14, 2024, https://en.wikipedia.org/wiki/Civic_engagement#:~:text=Civic%20engagement%20includes%20communities%20working,the%20quality%20of%20the%20community

14.	Patterson, Nicholas, "What is Environmental Sustainability? Goals with Examples," Southern New Hampshire University, April 22, 2022, https://www.snhu.edu/about-us/newsroom/stem/what-is-environmental-sustainability

15.	"Human ecology," Wikipedia, accessed March 14, 2024, https://en.wikipedia.org/wiki/Human_ecology

16.	"Cooperation," *Oxford Learner's Dictionaries*, accessed August 23, 2023, https://www.oxfordlearnersdictionaries.com/us/definition/english/cooperation

17.   "Economy," Vocabulary.com, accessed August 23, 2023, https://www.vocabulary.com/dictionary/economy

18.   The Investopedia Team, "What Is a Market Economy and How Does It Work?" Investopedia, Updated April 7, 2022, https://www.investopedia.com/terms/m/marketeconomy.asp

19.   "Mixed economy," Oxford Reference, accessed August 23, 2023, https://www.oxfordreference.com/view/10.1093/oi/authority.20110803100202353

20.   This definition combines the definitions of "cooperation" and "economy."

21.   "Chimpanzee Society," Project R and R, accessed August 23, 2023, https://releasechimps.org/chimpanzees/chimpanzee-society

22.   Ibid.

23.   Cohen-Brown, Brittany, "From top to bottom, chimpanzees social hierarchy is amazing!" *Jane Goodall's Good for All News,* July 10, 2018, https://news.janegoodall.org/2018/07/10/top-bottom-chimpanzee-social-hierarchy-amazing/

24.   Pryor, Frederic L., "A Survey Of The Economic Systems Of Wild Chimpanzees And Baboons," Swarthmore College, March 1, 1981, https://works.swarthmore.edu/cgi/viewcontent.cgi?article=1180&context=fac-economics

25.   Ibid.

26.   Laberge, Maxine, "Bears, Chimps, Humans and Monkeys: What's the difference?" *Jane Goodall's Good for All News,* June 27, 2018, https://news.janegoodall.org/2018/06/27/chimps-humans-monkeys-whats-difference/

27.   Mora-Bermudez, Felipe et al, "Differences and similarities between human and chimpanzee neural progenitors during cerebral cortex development," Max Planck Institute of Molecular Cell Biology and Genetics, Germany, September 26, 2016, https://elifesciences.org/articles/18683

28. Nuwer, Rachel, "Chimps Have an Innate Sense of Fairness," *Smithsonian*, January 16, 2013, https://www.smithsonianmag.com/smart-news/chimps-have-an-innate-sense-of-fairness-1901948/

29. Helper, Reed, "What is a Potlatch?" Study.com, accessed August 24, 2023, https://study.com/academy/lesson/native-american-potlatch-ceremony-definition-lesson-quiz.html

30. "What monkeys can teach us about money," BBC Worklife, April 6, 2018, https://www.bbc.com/worklife/article/20180406-what-monkeys-can-teach-us-about-money

31. For example: Barras, op. cit. (Endnote 6)

32. Yong, Ed, "A Cultural Leap at the Dawn of Humanity," *The Atlantic,* March 15, 2018, https://www.theatlantic.com/science/archive/2018/03/a-deeper-origin-of-complex-human-cultures/555674/

33. Ibid.

34. Ibid.

35. Ibid.

36. Wilford, John Noble, "When Humans Became Human," *New York Times*, February 26, 2002, https://www.nytimes.com/2002/02/26/science/when-humans-became-human.html#:~:text=The%20first%20human%20ancestors%20appeared,after%20two%20million%20years%20ago. 4

37. "Early human migration," Wikipedia, accessed August 24, 2023, https://en.wikipedia.org/wiki/Early_human_migrations#:~:text=Dispersal%20throughout%20Africa,-Further%20information%3A%20Macro&text=Homo%20sapiens%20are%20believed%20to,%2C%20Morocco%2C%20published%20in%202017.

38. Joyce, Christopher, "What Drove Early Man Across Globe? Climate Change," National Public Radio, September 17, 2012, https://www.npr.org/2012/09/17/161278993/what-drove-early-man-across-globe-climate-change

39. Hunt, Katie, "Early humans left Africa and reached Asia earlier than thought, fossil discovery reveals," CNN, June 14, 2023, https://www.cnn.com/2023/06/13/asia/laos-cave-early-human-fossils-scn/index.html

40. Kaneda, Toshiko and Carl Haub, "How Many People Have Ever Lived on Earth?" Population Reference Bureau, November 15, 2022, https://www.prb.org/articles/how-many-people-have-ever-lived-on-earth/

41. "What does it mean to have Neanderthal or Denisovan DNA?" MedlinePlus, accessed August 25, 2023, https://medlineplus.gov/genetics/understanding/dtcgenetictesting/neanderthaldna/

42. Ungar, Laura and Maddie Burakoff, "We carry DNA from extinct cousins like Neanderthals. Science is now revealing their genetic legacy," The Associated Press, updated September 27, 2023, https://apnews.com/article/neanderthals-denisovans-genetics-dna-disease-e49cb7d939cfe5d583e7ed0af8751784

43. Ashworth, James, "Oldest evidence of modern humans in western Europe discovered," Natural History Museum, London, February 9, 2022, https://www.nhm.ac.uk/discover/news/2022/february/oldest-evidence-modern-humans-western-europe-discovered.html#:~:text=A%20single%20tooth%20found%20in,significantly%20earlier%20than%20previously%20known.

44. Dorey, Fran, "When did modern humans get to Australia?" Australian Museum, updated December 9, 2021, https://australian.museum/learn/science/human-evolution/the-spread-of-people-to-australia/

45. Ibid.

46. Rincon, Paul, "Earliest evidence for humans in the Americas," BBC News, July 22, 2020, https://www.bbc.com/news/science-environment-53486868

47. Prates, Luciano et al, "Rapid radiation of humans in South America after the last glacial maximum: A radiocarbon-based study," *Plos One*, published online July 22, 2020, https://journals.plos.org/plosone/article?id=10.1371/journal.pone.0236023

48.   "History of Oceania," Wikipedia, accessed August 25, 2023, https://en.wikipedia.org/wiki/History_of_Oceania

49.   Plackett, Benjamin, "How many early human species existed on Earth?" *LiveScience,* January 24, 2021, https://www.livescience.com/how-many-human-species.html

50.   Zimmer, Carl, "How the First Farmers Changed History," *New York Times,* October 17, 2016, https://www.nytimes.com/2016/10/18/science/ancient-farmers-archaeology-dna.html

51.   *Proceedings of the National Academy of Sciences,* April 22, 2014, https://www.pnas.org/doi/10.1073/pnas.1323964111

52.   Kennedy, Lesley, "The Prehistoric Ages: How Humans Lived Before Written Records," History, updated June 9, 2023, https://www.history.com/news/prehistoric-ages-timeline#

53.   Ibid.

54.   Wells, Peter, "Weapons, Ritual and Warfare: Violence in Iron Age Europe," Cambridge Core, March 13, 2020, https://www.cambridge.org/core/books/abs/cambridge-world-history-of-violence/weapons-ritual-and-warfare-violence-in-iron-age-europe/CE09A5882FA1AD8C173403764754F0D0

55.   Mercader, Julio, "Mozambican Grass Seed Consumption During the Middle Stone Age," *Science,* Volume 326, Issue 5960, pp. 1680-2009, December 18, 2009, https://pubmed.ncbi.nlm.nih.gov/20019285/

56.   "History of agriculture," Wikipedia, accessed August 29, 2023, https://en.wikipedia.org/wiki/History_of_agriculture#Sumer

57.   "Food production, history of," Encyclopedia.com, accessed August 29, 2023, https://www.encyclopedia.com/food/encyclopedias-almanacs-transcripts-and-maps/food-production-history

Endnotes

58. "Origins of agriculture: Year of China," Brown University,
     accessed August 29, 2023, https://www.brown.edu/
     about/administration/international-affairs/year-of-china/
     origins-agriculture-china-hunting-and-gathering-early-farming

59. Kingwell-Banham, Eleanor et al, "Early agriculture in South Asia,"
     Cambridge University Press, May 5, 2015, https://www.cambridge.org/
     core/books/abs/cambridge-world-history/early-agriculture-in-south-asia/
     4614A6BF7F642A488592CA802902F671

60. Cothrin, E. Gus, "Origin of horse domestication," *Encyclopedia Britannica,*
     accessed August 29, 2023, https://www.britannica.com/animal/horse/
     Origin-of-horse-domestication

61. "Domestication of the horse," Wikipedia, accessed August 29, 2023,
     https://en.wikipedia.org/wiki/Domestication_of_the_
     horse#:~:text=Genetic%20evidence%20indicates%20that%20
     domestication,%2C%20agricultural%20work%2C%20and%20warfare.

62. "Agriculture in Papua New Guinea," Wikipedia, accessed August 29, 2023,
     https://en.wikipedia.org/wiki/Agriculture_in_Papua_New_Guinea

63. Doughty, Christopher E., "The development of agriculture in the Americas:
     an ecological perspective," *Ecosphere,* December 28, 2010, https://
     esajournals.onlinelibrary.wiley.com/doi/full/10.1890/ES10-00098.1

64. Gray, Alic William et al, "Origins of agriculture: The Americas," *Encyclopedia
     Britannica,* updated August 21, 2023, https://www.britannica.com/topic/
     agriculture/The-Americas

65. Baker, David, "The Origin Of Agriculture In Africa," Khan Academy,
     accessed August 29, 2023, https://www.khanacademy.org/humanities/
     big-history-project/agriculture-civilization/first-cities-appear/a/
     the-origin-of-agriculture-in-africa#:~:text=Eventually%2C%20
     however%2C%20West%20Africans%20began,of%20rice%20native%20
     to%20Africa

66. "Indigenous Australians farmed bananas 2,000 years ago," *BBC News,*
     August 12, 2020, https://www.bbc.com/news/world-australia-53746652

67. "Aboriginal land management and care," Creative Spirits, accessed March 19, 2024, https://www.creativespirits.info/aboriginalculture/land/aboriginal-land-care

68. Wong, Kate, "Why Is *Homo sapiens* the Sole Surviving Member of the Human Family? Recent fossil, archaeological and genetic discoveries are revising the rise of our species," *Scientific American*, September 1, 2018, https://www.scientificamerican.com/article/why-is-homo-sapiens-the-sole-surviving-member-of-the-human-family/#:~:text=By%20around%2040%2C000%20years%20ago,sapiens%20and%20its%20extinct%20relatives.)

69. Nadeau, E.G. and Luc Nadeau, *The Cooperative Society: The Next Stage of Human History, Second Edition,* The Cooperative Society Project, 2018, https://thecooperativesociety.org/book-the-cooperative-society/

70. Goldewijk, Kees Klein et al, "Long term dynamic modeling of global population and built-up area in a spatially explicit way," Hyde (History Database of the Global Environment), PBL Netherlands Environmental Assessment Agency, June 2010, https://www.researchgate.net/publication/228074776_Long_term_dynamic_modeling_of_global_population_and_built-up_area_in_a_spatially_explicit_way_HYDE_31

71. "Estimates of historical world population," Wikipedia, accessed March 19, 2024, https://en.wikipedia.org/wiki/Estimates_of_historical_world_population

72. Pennington, R. L., "Causes of early human population growth," *American Journal of Physiological Anthropology,* February 1996, https://pubmed.ncbi.nlm.nih.gov/8967327/

73. "Prehistoric populations," Encyclopedia.com, accessed September 23, 2023, https://www.encyclopedia.com/social-sciences/encyclopedias-almanacs-transcripts-and-maps/prehistoric-populations

74. Renfrew, Colin, "Inception of agriculture and rearing in the Middle East," *Human Palaeontology and Prehistory,* 2006, https://www.sciencedirect.com/science/article/pii/S163106830500134X

Endnotes

75. Grabmeier, Jeff, "9,000 years ago, a community with modern
     urban problems," *Ohio State News,* June 2019, https://news.osu.
     edu/9000-years-ago-a-community-with-modern-urban-problems/

76. "Greek city states," *National Geographic Education,* May 20, 2022, https://
     education.nationalgeographic.org/resource/greek-city-states/#

77. Martin, Kevin, "The Age of Greece: Rise and Decline of
     the Ancient Greek City-States," Magellan, September
     28, 2018, https://www.magellantv.com/articles/
     the-age-of-greece-rise-and-decline-of-the-ancient-greek-citystates

78. Mark, Joshua J., "Sumerians," World Historical Encyclopedia,
     October 9, 2019, https://www.worldhistory.org/Sumerians/

79. Ibid.

80. Ibid.

81. The Conversation, "Akkadia: How Climate Change Doomed The World's
     First Empire," The Conversation, July 1, 2019, https://theconversation.
     com/how-climate-change-caused-the-worlds-first-ever-empire-to-
     collapse-109060#:~:text=The%20anguish%20of%20the%20era,thick%20
     clouds%20did%20not%20rain.

82. Alejandrino, Jonnel, "The Akkadian Empire," Scribd, accessed
     August 25, 2023, https://www.scribd.com/document/326441457/
     The-Akkadian-Empire

83. "Akkadian Empire," Wikipedia, accessed September 3, 2023, https://
     en.wikipedia.org/wiki/Akkadian_Empire

84. The Conversation, op. cit. (Endnote 81)

85. Ibid

86. "Empire," *Oxford Learners Dictionaries,* accessed September 3, 2023,
     https://www.oxfordlearnersdictionaries.com/us/definition/
     american_english/empire

87. "Roman Empire," Wikipedia, accessed September 3, 2023, https://en.wikipedia.org/wiki/Roman_Empire#/media/File:Roman_Empire_Trajan_117AD.png

88. "Classical demography," Wikipedia, accessed September 3, 2023, https://en.wikipedia.org/wiki/Classical_demography

89. "Dynasties in Chinese history," Wikipedia, accessed September 3, 2023, https://en.wikipedia.org/wiki/Dynasties_in_Chinese_historyhttps://en.wikipedia.org/wiki/History_of_trade_of_the_People%27s_Republic_of_China#History_of_Chinese_foreign_trade

90. "Mauryan Empire," *Encyclopedia Britannica,* accessed September 3, 2023, https://www.britannica.com/place/Mauryan-Empire

91. "Countries alongside silk road routes/India," UNESCO, accessed September 3, 2023, https://en.unesco.org/silkroad/countries-alongside-silk-road-routes/india

92. Christensen, Brandon, "10 Southeast Asian Kingdoms You Need to Know About," Real Clear History, November 15, 2018, https://www.realclearhistory.com/articles/2018/11/15/10_southeast_asian_kingdoms_you_need_to_know_about_385.html

93. "South-Eastern Asia Population," Worldometers, November 15, 2018, https://www.worldometers.info/world-population/south-eastern-asia-population/

94. Christensen, op.cit. (Endnote 92)

95. Gitonga, Ruth and Cyprine Apindi, "10 famous and powerful African kingdoms, empires, and civilizations," Briefly," updated April 2023, https://briefly.co.za/78031-10-famous-powerful-african-kingdoms-about.html

96. "Trans-Saharan trade," Wikipedia, accessed September 3, 2023, https://en.wikipedia.org/wiki/Trans-Saharan_trade

97. "Organization of Genghis Khan's empire," *Encyclopedia Britannica,* accessed September 3, 2023, https://www.britannica.com/place/Mongol-empire/Organization-of-Genghis-Khans-empire ;

98. "Destruction under the Mongol Empire," Wikipedia, accessed September 3, 2023, https://en.wikipedia.org/wiki/Destruction_under_the_Mongol_Empire

99. "Agriculture in Papua New Guinea," Wikipedia, accessed September 3, 2023, https://en.wikipedia.org/wiki/Agriculture_in_Papua_New_Guinea

100. Winn, Patrick, "Papuan tribal leaders to author Jared Diamond: 'Don't call us warlike,'" *GlobalPost*, February 18, 2013, https://theworld.org/stories/2013-02-18/papuan-tribal-leaders-author-jared-diamond-don-t-call-us-warlike

101. Harding, Thomas G., "Precolonial New Guinea Trade," University of Pittsburgh of the Commonwealth System of Higher Education, Spring 1994, https://www.jstor.org/stable/3773892

102. Jorari, Leanne, "PNG: Mistaking massacres for tradition in Papua New Guinea's Hela province," Lowy Institute, February 9, 2021, https://www.lowyinstitute.org/the-interpreter/png-mistaking-massacres-tradition

103. "Caral-Supe civilization," Wikipedia, accessed September 3, 2023, https://en.wikipedia.org/wiki/Caral-Supe_civilization

104. "Central and South American Empires," UShistory.org, accessed September 3, 2023, https://www.ushistory.org/civ/11.asp

105. "Regional communications in ancient Mesoamerica," Wikipedia, accessed September 3, 2023, https://en.wikipedia.org/wiki/Regional_communications_in_ancient_Mesoamerica#:~:text=There%20are%20numerous%20evidences%20of,strong%20possibility%2C%20based%20on%20evidences.

106. "How agriculture and domestication began: The Americas," *Encyclopedia Britannica*, accessed September 3, 2023, https://www.britannica.com/topic/agriculture/The-Americas

107. Jarus, Owen, "Cahokia: North America's First City," LiveScience, January 11, 2018, https://www.livescience.com/22737-cahokia.html

108. Chacon, Richard J. and Ruben G. Mendoza (Editors,) *North American Indigenous Warfare and Ritual Violence,* University of Arizona Press, 2013, https://uapress.arizona.edu/book/north-american-indigenous-warfare-and-ritual-violence

109. "British Empire," National archives (United Kingdom), archived on February 22, 2022, https://www.nationalarchives.gov.uk/education/empire/g1/cs4/background.htm

110. "Australian frontier wars," Wikipedia, accessed September 4, 2023, https://en.wikipedia.org/wiki/Australian_frontier_wars

111. "Aboriginal Art & Culture," Alice Springs, Australia, accessed September 4, 2023, https://www.aboriginalart.com.au/culture/trade.html

112. "Black Death," History.com, accessed September 4, 2023, https://www.history.com/topics/middle-ages/black-death

113. "Pandemics That Changed History," History.com, accessed September 4, 2023, https://www.history.com/topics/middle-ages/pandemics-timeline

114. "Prince Henry the Navigator," Wikipedia, accessed March 21, 2024, https://en.wikipedia.org/wiki/Prince_Henry_the_Navigator

115. Rodrigue, Jean-Paul, *The Geography of Transport Systems,* Sixth edition, Routledge, 2006, https://transportgeography.org/contents/chapter1/emergence-of-mechanized-transportation-systems/spanish-portuguese-empires-17th-century/#:~:text=By%20treaty%20(Tordesillas%2C%20 1494%20and,the%20Treaty%20of%20Zaragoza%20was

116. "Rivalry Between English and Dutch East India Companies," World History Commons, accessed September 4, 2023, https://worldhistorycommons.org/rivalry-between-english-and-dutch-east-india-companies

117. "East India Company," Wikipedia, accessed September 4, 2023, https://en.wikipedia.org/wiki/East_India_Company

118. "Industrial Revolution," Wikipedia, accessed September 4, 2023, https://en.wikipedia.org/wiki/Industrial_Revolution

119. Rafferty, John P., "The Rise of the Machines: Pros and Cons of the Industrial Revolution," *Encyclopedia Britannica*, accessed April 11, 2024, https://www.britannica.com/story/the-rise-of-the-machines-pros-and-cons-of-the-industrial-revolution#:~:text=Con%3A%20Overcrowding%20of%20Cities%20and%20Industrial%20Towns&text=People%20living%20in%20such%20close,tuberculosis%2C%20and%20other%20infectious%20diseases.

120. "Territorial Gains by the U.S.," National Geographic Education, accessed September 4, 2023, https://education.nationalgeographic.org/resource/territorial-gains/#

121. Munson, Olivia, "What is the biggest state in the US? The states from largest to smallest by land area," *USA Today*, updated August 8, 2023, https://www.usatoday.com/story/news/2022/12/09/what-largest-state-us-size-states-land-area/8083288001/#

122. "American War of Independence: Outbreak," National Army Museum, accessed September 4, 2023, https://www.nam.ac.uk/explore/american-war-independence-outbreak#:~:text=13%20colonies&text=Most%20were%20created%20by%20emigrants,kilometres%20(430%2C000%20square%20miles)

123. "U.S. Population Estimated at 334,233,854," US Census Bureau, January 2023, https://www.census.gov/library/stories/2022/12/happy-new-year-2023.html#:~:text=U.S.%20Population%20Estimated%20at%20334%2C233%2C854%20on%20Jan.&text=1%2C%202023.,1%20person%20every%2027%20seconds

124. "American imperialism," Wikipedia, accessed September 04, 2023, https://en.wikipedia.org/wiki/American_imperialism

125. "Millennium Development Goals (MDGs)," World Health Organization, February 19, 2018, https://www.who.int/news-room/fact-sheets/detail/millennium-development-goals-(mdgs)#:~:text=The%20United%20Nations%20Millennium%20Declaration,are%20derived%20from%20this%20Declaration

126. "Capitalism," *Oxford Learner's Dictionaries,* accessed August 10, 2023, (https://www.oxfordlearnersdictionaries.com/us/definition/english/capitalism)

127. "Homo economicus," Wikipedia, accessed August 10, 2023, (https://en.wikipedia.org/wiki/Homo_economicus)

128. "Liberalism," Wikipedia, accessed September 29, 2023, https://en.wikipedia.org/wiki/Liberalism

129. "Socialism," National Geographic Education, accessed August 10, 2023, https://education.nationalgeographic.org/resource/socialism/#

130. Shin, Hyonhee, "Private sector overtakes state as North Korea's top economic actor under Kim," Reuters, December 16, 2021, https://www.reuters.com/markets/asia/private-sector-overtakes-state-north-koreas-top-economic-actor-under-kim-skorea-2021-12-16/

131. "Communism," Oxford Learner's Dictionaries, accessed August 10, 2023, https://www.oxfordlearnersdictionaries.com/us/definition/american_english/communism

132. "Communism," National Geographic Education, accessed August 10, 2023, https://education.nationalgeographic.org/resource/communism/#

133. "Who Killed More: Hitler, Stalin, or Mao?" ChinaFile, February 5, 2018, https://www.chinafile.com/library/nyrb-china-archive/who-killed-more-hitler-stalin-or-mao

134. "Mixed economy," Oxford Reference, accessed August 10, 2023, https://www.oxfordreference.com/view/10.1093/oi/authority.20110803100202353

135. This definition combines the definitions of "cooperation" and "economy."

136. "Co-operative economics," Wikipedia, accessed August 10, 2023, https://
en.wikipedia.org/wiki/Co-operative_economics#:~:text=Cooperative%20
Economics%20as%20an%20Alternative%20to%20Market%20
Societies,-Jessica%2DGordon%20Nembhard&text=use%20a%20
sense%20of%20solidarity,help%20stabilize%20their%20economic%20
circumstances

137. "Charge of the Intercontinental Network of the Social Solidarity Economy
(RIPESS)," RIPESS, accessed August 10, 2023, https://www.ripess.org/
wp-content/uploads/2017/08/RIPESS_charter_EN.pdf

138. Intergovernmental Organizations (IGOs), Harvard Law School,
accessed September 13, 2023, https://hls.harvard.edu/
bernard-koteen-office-of-public-interest-advising/about-
opia/what-is-public-interest-law/public-service-practice-
settings/international-public-interest-law-practice-setting/
intergovernmental-organizations-igos/

139. "List of intergovernmental organizations," Wikipedia,
accessed October 3, 2023, https://en.wikipedia.org/wiki/
List_of_intergovernmental_organizations

140. "United Nations Charter, Chapter I: Purposes and Principles, Article
1," United Nations, signed on June 26, 1945, https://www.un.org/en/
about-us/un-charter/chapter-1

141. "UN's mission 'more important than ever', Secretary-General says at UN
Day ceremony," UN News, October 26, 2020, https://news.un.org/en/
story/2020/10/1076142

142. Ibid.

143. "Sustainable development goals" World Health Organization –
Europe, March 22, 2024, https://www.who.int/europe/about-us/
our-work/sustainable-development-goals#:~:text=Section%20
navigation&text=The%20Sustainable%20Development%20Goals%20
(SDGs,enjoy%20health%2C%20justice%20and%20prosperity.

144. *The Millennium Development Goals Report 2015,* United Nations, accessed October 3, 2023, https://www.un.org/millenniumgoals/2015_MDG_Report/pdf/MDG%202015%20rev%20(July%201).pdf

145. *The Sustainable Development Goals Report 2023: Special Edition,* United Nations, accessed October 3, 2023, https://unstats.un.org/sdgs/report/2023/

146. "The Paris Agreement," United Nations: Climate Action, accessed October 3, 2023, https://www.un.org/en/climatechange/paris-agreement

147. "Peace, dignity and equality on a healthy planet," United Nations, accessed October 3, 2023, https://www.un.org/en/global-issues/democracy#:~:text=Democracy%20in%20the%20founding%20documents%20of%20the%20United%20Nations&text=The%20UN%20does%20not%20advocate,equality%2C%20security%20and%20human%20development.

148. "Department of Economic and Social Affairs: Cooperatives," United Nations, accessed October 10, 2023, https://www.un.org/development/desa/cooperatives/what-we-do.html

149. "Aims and values," European Union, accessed March 22, 2024, https://european-union.europa.eu/principles-countries-history/principles-and-values/aims-and-values_en

150. *Democracy Index 2023: Age of Conflict,* Economist Intelligence Unit, February 15, 2024, https://www.eiu.com/n/campaigns/democracy-index-2023/?utm_source=eiu-website&utm_medium=blog&utm_campaign=democracy-index-2023

151. "Brexit–new EU-UK partnership: where do we stand?," access date, Government of the Netherlands, December 24, 2020, https://www.government.nl/topics/brexit/brexit-where-do-we-stand

152. "Viktor Orban's far right vision for Europe," *The New Yorker,* January 14, 2019, https://www.newyorker.com/magazine/2019/01/14/viktor-orbans-far-right-vision-for-europe

153. Koenen, Krisztina, "Hungary and the EU: A deepening divide," GIS Reports, May 17, 2023, https://www.gisreportsonline.com/r/hungary-eu-divide/

154. Casert, Raf, "EU moves to end standoff with Poland over anti-EU policies and begins to release billions in funds," The Associated Press, February 29, 2024, https://apnews.com/article/eu-commission-poland-frozen-funds-release-e1e4bfa42a371fb45fcf7b5a1948224b#

155. "Estimated number of refugees from Ukraine recorded in Europe and Asia since February 2022 as of July 11, 2023, by selected country," Statista Research Department, September 7, 2023, https://www.statista.com/statistics/1312584/ukrainian-refugees-by-country/

156. "European social model," Wikipedia, accessed October 3, 2023, https://en.wikipedia.org/wiki/European_social_model

157. "European green deal: Fit for 55," European Council, accessed October 7, 2023, https://www.consilium.europa.eu/en/policies/green-deal/fit-for-55-the-eu-plan-for-a-green-transition/

158. *Democracy Index 2023*, op. cit. (Endnote 150)

159. "The World Bank in Botswana," The World Bank, accessed October 7, 2023, https://www.worldbank.org/en/country/botswana/overview

160. "What is a carbon sink?" ClientEarth, December 22, 2020, https://www.clientearth.org/latest/latest-updates/stories/what-is-a-carbon-sink/#:~:text=A%20carbon%20sink%20is%20anything,fossil%20fuels%20or%20volcanic%20eruptions

161. "Botswana," Global Forest Watch, accessed March 14, 2024, https://www.globalforestwatch.org/dashboards/country/BWA/?category=climate&location=WyJjb3VudHJ5IiwiQldBIl0%3D#

162. "Botswana: Climate risk country profile," Reliefweb, January 18, 2021, https://reliefweb.int/report/botswana/botswana-climate-risk-country-profile

163. *Democracy Index 2023*, op. cit. (Endnote 150)

164. "Costa Rica," *OECD Better Life Index*, accessed March 14, 2024, https://www.oecdbetterlifeindex.org/countries/costa-rica/

165. "Costa Rica Leads the Way in Cutting Carbon Emissions," *Rand Review*, August 30, 2021, https://www.rand.org/blog/rand-review/2021/08/costa-rica-leads-the-way-in-cutting-carbon-emissions.html

166. *Democracy Index 2023*, op. cit. (Endnote 150)

167. "Iceland," *OECD Better Life Index*, accessed March 14, 2024, https://www.oecdbetterlifeindex.org/countries/iceland/

168. "Climate change," Government of Iceland, accessed March 14, 2024 https://www.government.is/topics/environment-climate-and-nature-protection/climate-change/

169. "Kiribati," Wikipedia, accessed March 14, 2024, https://en.wikipedia.org/wiki/Kiribati

170. "Kiribati," *Freedom in the World 2023*, Freedom House, accessed March 14, 2024, https://freedomhouse.org/country/kiribati/freedom-world/2023

171. "Kiribati," Wikipedia, accessed March 14, 2024, https://en.wikipedia.org/wiki/Kiribati

172. "Kiribati and China to develop former climate-refuge land in Fiji," Island Innovation, March 3, 2021, https://islandinnovation.co/news/kiribati-and-china-to-develop-former-climate-refuge-land-in-fiji/

173. "Kiribati climate change policy," Republic of Kiribati, April 2019, https://www.president.gov.ki/presidentgovki/wp-content/uploads/2019/04/Kiribati-Climate-Change-Policy.pdf

174. *Democracy Index 2023*, op. cit. (Endnote 150)

175. "OECD Better Life Index: Korea," *OECD Better Life Index*, accessed October 7, 2023, https://www.oecdbetterlifeindex.org/countries/korea/

176. "South Korea aims to cut carbon emissions by 40% in 2030,"
The Associated Press, October 18, 2021, https://apnews.com/
article/climate-change-business-europe-scotland-moon-jae-in-
847cba4f6c6be815489f722c2b5a256a

177. International Cooperative Alliance, op. cit. (Endnote 11)

178. EURICSE: Knowledge for a Social Economy," Euricse, accessed
October 11, 2023, https://euricse.eu/en/

179. *Exploring the cooperative economy: Report 2022,* World Cooperative
Monitor, accessed October 11, 2023, https://monitor.coop/en/
media/library/research-and-reviews-world-cooperative-monitor/
world-cooperative-monitor-2022

180. Dave Grace and Associates, "Measuring the Size and Scope of
the Cooperative Economy: Results of the 2014 Global Census on
Co-operatives," For the United Nation's Secretariat, Department of
Economic and Social Affairs, Division for Social Policy and Development,
April 2014, https://www.un.org/esa/socdev/documents/2014/
coopsegm/grace.pdf

181. "Cooperative enterprises build a better world," International Cooperative
Alliance, accessed October 11, 2023, https://www.ica.coop/en/about-us/
International-cooperative-alliance

182. The Investopedia Team, "What Is Environmental, Social, and Governance
(ESG) Investing?" Investopedia, updated February 06, 2024, https://www.
investopedia.com/terms/e/environmental-social-and-governance-esg-
criteria.asp

183. "Environmental, social and corporate governance," Wikipedia,
accessed March 14, 2024, https://en.wikipedia.org/wiki/
Environmental,_social,_and_corporate_governance

184. The Investopedia Team, op. cit. (Endnote 182)

185. Hayes, Adam, "What Is Greenwashing? How It Works, Examples, and
Statistics," Investopedia, January 22, 2024, https://www.investopedia.com/
terms/g/greenwashing.asp

186. "Non-profit organizations," Legal information Institute, Cornell Law School, accessed March 14, 2024, https://www.law.cornell.edu/wex/non-profit_organizations

187. Reasonover, Charles, "50 Nonprofit Facts and Statistics," September 6, 2021, https://www.501c3.org/50-nonprofit-facts-and-statistics/

188. NCCS Project Team, "The Nonprofit Sector in Brief 2019," Urban Institute, June 2020, https://urbaninstitute.github.io/nccs-legacy/briefs/sector-brief-2019

189. "Charity and Disaster Fraud," FBI, accessed March 14, 2024, https://www.fbi.gov/how-we-can-help-you/scams-and-safety/common-scams-and-crimes/charity-and-disaster-fraud#

190. Vogel, Kenneth P. and Shane Goldmacher, "An Unusual $1.6 Billion Donation Bolsters Conservatives," *New York Times,* August 22, 2022,

191. "Fridays for Future," Fridays for Future, accessed October 11, 2023, https://fridaysforfuture.org

192. Dadouch, Sarah, "Greta Thunberg holds last school strike as climate activist graduates," *Washington Post,* June 9, 2023, https://www.washingtonpost.com/world/2023/06/09/greta-thunberg-graduation-climate-strike/

193. Hassan, Jennifer, "Greta Thunberg says world leaders' talk on climate change is 'blah blah blah,'" September 29, 2021, https://www.washingtonpost.com/climate-environment/2021/09/29/great-thunberg-leaders-blah-blah-blah/

194. "Bhutan," Wikipedia, accessed March 17, 2024, https://en.wikipedia.org/wiki/Bhutan

195. *Democracy Index 2023,* op. cit. (Endnote 150)

196. Ibid.

197. Mithen, Steven J., "Thoughtful Foragers: A Study of Prehistoric Decision Making," *New Studies in Archaeology* (First Edition), Cambridge University Press, online publication date: August 2010, https://www.cambridge.org/core/books/thoughtful-foragers/7F2BB38603FB9B8CFD24E13EE8CC717B

198. Conradt, L. and T.J. Roper, "Democracy in animals: the evolution of shared group decisions," Proceedings of The Royal Society B: Biological Sciences, published online July 20, 2007, https://www.ncbi.nlm.nih.gov/pmc/articles/PMC2288530/

199. For example: "Democracy (Ancient Greece)," National Geographic: Education, accessed October 12, 2023, https://education.nationalgeographic.org/resource/democracy-ancient-greece/

200. Declaration of Independence: A Transcription, America's Founding Documents, accessed March 17, 2024, https://www.archives.gov/founding-docs/declaration-transcript

201. http://www.historyworld.net/wrldhis/PlainTextHistories.asp?ParagraphID=mzs

202. https://en.wikipedia.org/wiki/Iroquois

203. "Taxation Without Representation: What It Means and History," Julia Kagan, Investopedia, updated February 15, 2024, https://www.investopedia.com/terms/t/tax_without_representation.asp#:~:text=The%20phrase%20taxation%20without%20representation,1

204. "Constitution of the United States," Wikipedia, accessed March 17, 2024, https://en.wikipedia.org/wiki/Constitution_of_the_United_States

205. "Why do states have different election rules? (2022)," Ballotpedia, accessed March 17, 2024, https://ballotpedia.org/Why_do_states_have_different_election_rules%3F_(2022)

206. Infoplease Staff, "U.S. State Population by Rank (Update for 2023!)," Infoplease, updated July 21, 2023, https://www.infoplease.com/us/states/state-population-by-rank

207. "List of United States presidential elections in which the winner lost the popular vote," Wikipedia, accessed March 17, 2024, https://en.wikipedia.org/wiki/List_of_United_States_presidential_elections_in_which_the_winner_lost_the_popular_vote

208. "European colonization of the Americas," Wikipedia, March 17, 2024, https://en.wikipedia.org/wiki/European_colonization_of_the_Americas

209. Kent, Lauren, "European colonizers killed so many Native Americans that it changed the global climate, researchers say," CNN, February 2, 2019, https://www.cnn.com/2019/02/01/world/european-colonization-climate-change-trnd/index.html#:~:text=European%20settlers%20killed%2056%20million,London%2C%20or%20UCL%2C%20estimate.

210. "August 20, 1619: First enslaved Africans arrive in Jamestown, setting the stage for slavery in North America," accessed March 17, 2024, https://www.history.com/this-day-in-history/first-african-slave-ship-arrives-jamestown-colony#

211. "The Emancipation Proclamation," National Archives, accessed March 17, 2024, https://www.archives.gov/exhibits/featured-documents/emancipation-proclamation

212. Williams, Noelle Lorraine, "New Jersey, The Last Northern State to End Slavery," New Jersey Historical Commission, accessed March 17, 2024, https://nj.gov/state/historical/his-2021-juneteenth.shtml

213. "Reconstruction and Its Impact," State Historical Society of Iowa, accessed March 17, 2024, https://history.iowa.gov/history/education/educator-resources/primary-source-sets/reconstruction-and-its-impact#:~:text=The%20Reconstruction%20Era%20lasted%20from,between%20African%20Americans%20and%20whites.

214. Landwehr, Aimee, "What ended Reconstruction in 1877?" accessed March 17, 2024, https://study.com/academy/lesson/the-end-of-reconstruction-and-the-election-of-1876.html#:~:text=While%20many%20factors%20led%20to,over%20race%2C%20and%20economic%20difficulties.

215. "Indentured servitude," Wikipedia, accessed March 17, 2024, https://en.wikipedia.org/wiki/Indentured_servitude

216. "Corruption in the United States," Wikipedia, accessed March 17, 2024, https://en.wikipedia.org/wiki/Corruption_in_the_United_States

217. Graham, David A., "The Cases Against Trump: A Guide," *The Atlantic*, February 15, 2024, https://www.theatlantic.com/ideas/archive/2024/02/donald-trump-legal-cases-charges/675531/

218. "Foreign interventions by the United States," Wikipedia, accessed March 17, 2024, " https://en.wikipedia.org/wiki/Foreign_interventions_by_the_United_States

219. Shamn, Scott, "Russia Isn't the Only One Meddling in Elections. We Do It, Too." *New York Times,* February 17, 2018, https://www.nytimes.com/2018/02/17/sunday-review/russia-isnt-the-only-one-meddling-in-elections-we-do-it-too.html

220. Trenta, Luca, "The US has blurred the lines on assassination for decades," The Conversation, August 26, 2016, https://theconversation.com/the-us-has-blurred-the-lines-on-assassination-for-decades-63622

221. Bhalerao, Anandita, "Former President Trump found guilty on all 34 felony charges in hush money trial," NPR, May 31, 2024, https://www.npr.org/2024/05/31/g-s1-2086/former-president-trump-found-guilty-on-all-34-felony-charges-in-hush-money-trial

222. "The Amendments," The National Constitution Center, accessed March 17, 2024, https://constitutioncenter.org/the-constitution/amendments

223. DesJardins, Jeff, "Mapped: The world's oldest democracies," World Economic Forum, August 8, 2019, https://www.weforum.org/agenda/2019/08/countries-are-the-worlds-oldest-democracies/

224. "The Polity Project," Center for Systemic Peace, accessed March 24, 2024, https://www.systemicpeace.org/polityproject.html

225. Ibid.

226. Ibid.

227. *Democracy Index 2023,* op. cit. (Endnote 150)

228. *Freedom in the World 2024*, Freedom House, February 2024, https://freedomhouse.org/sites/default/files/2024-02/FIW_2024_DigitalBooklet.pdf

229. *Democracy Index 2023*, op. cit. (Endnote 150)

230. *Freedom in the World 2024*, op. cit. (Endnote 228)

231. Nadeau, E.G., "Democracy Is Making A Comeback!," The Cooperative Society Project, March 26, 2022, https://thecooperativesociety.org/2022/03/26/democracy-is-making-a-comeback%EF%BF%BC/

232. Riccardi, Nicholas, "Democracy's appeal is slipping as nations across much of the world hold elections, a poll finds," The Associated Press, February 28, 2024, https://apnews.com/article/global-democracy-poll-government-politics-autocracy-bad95f3d53d0bb2c8d244f344654d1c7

233. "The Arab Spring country by country," *The National News*, June 16, 2011, https://www.thenationalnews.com/world/the-arab-spring-country-by-country-1.401358

234. Salem, Paul, "Why the Arab Spring Failed – And Why It May Yet Succeed," *Time*, January 5, 2021, https://time.com/5926292/arab-spring-future/

235. *Democracy Index 2023*, op. cit. (Endnote 150)

236. *Freedom in the World 2024*, op. cit. (Endnote 228)

237. *Democracy Index 2022*, "Frontline democracy and the battle for Ukraine," March 2, 2023, Economist Intelligence Unit, https://www.eiu.com/n/global-outlook-democracy-index-2022/

238. Ibid.

239. *Democracy Index 2023*, op. cit. (Endnote 150), "Freedom in the World 2024," op. cit. (Endnote 228)

240. "Total Population By Country 2024, World Population Review, accessed March 24, 2024, https://worldpopulationreview.com/countries

241. Salem, Paul, op. cit. (Endnote 234)

242. Vanheukelom, Jan, "Two years into South Africa's Just Energy Transition Partnership: How real is the deal?" Brief, European Centre for Development Policy Management, November 27, 2023, https://ecdpm. org/work/two-years-south-africas-just-energy-transition-partnership-how-real-deal#:~:text=heavy%20lifting%20ahead-,Summary,amount%20 of%20concessional%20climate%20finance

243. Kramer, Katherine, "Just Energy Transition Partnerships: An opportunity to leapfrog from coal to clean energy," International Institute For Sustainable Development, December 7, 2022, https://www.iisd.org/articles/insight/ just-energy-transition-partnerships

244. *Democracy Index 2023,* op. cit. (Endnote 150)

245. Ding, Iza and Dan Slater, "Democratic decoupling," Democratization, 28:1, 63-80, 2021, https://doi.org/10.1080/1 3510347.2020.1842361

246. *Democracy Index 2023,* op. cit. (Endnote 150)

247. Vollset, Stein et al, " Fertility, mortality, migration, and population scenarios for 195 countries and territories from 2017 to 2100: a forecasting analysis for the Global Burden of Disease Study," https://www. thelancet.com/journals/lancet/article/PIIS0140-6736(20)30677-2/fulltext

248. "List of countries by GDP (nominal) per capita," Wikipedia, accessed March 24,2024, https://en.wikipedia.org/wiki/ List_of_countries_by_GDP_(nominal)_per_capita

249. "Economic democracy," op. cit. (Endnote 9)

250. "Community Supported Agriculture," National Agricultural Library, US Department of Agriculture, accessed October 11, 2023, https:// www.nal.usda.gov/farms-and-agricultural-production-systems/ community-supported-agriculture

251. "Economic democracy," op. cit. (Endnote 9)

252. The Investopedia Team, "Labor Union: Definition, History, and Examples," Investopedia, updated September 14, 2022, https://www.investopedia. com/terms/l/labor-union.asp#:~:text=The%20Bottom%20Line-,A%20 labor%20union%20is%20an%20organization%20formed%20by%20 workers%20in,its%20behalf%20with%20the%20employer.

253. "About the ILO," International Labor Organization, accessed October 30, 2023, https://www.ilo.org/global/about-the-ilo/lang--en/index.htm

254. "Category: Workers' rights organizations," Wikipedia, accessed October 30, 2023, https://en.wikipedia.org/wiki/ Category:Workers%27_rights_organizations

255. "Consumer organization," Wikipedia, accessed October 30, 2023, https:// en.wikipedia.org/wiki/Consumer_organization#:~:text=Consumer%20 organizations%20are%20advocacy%20groups,litigation%2C%20 campaigning%2C%20or%20lobbying.

256. "National Labor Relations Board," Wikipedia, accessed October 30, 2023, https://en.wikipedia.org/wiki/National_Labor_Relations_Board

257. "Consumer protection laws," Cornell Law School, accessed October 30, 2023, https://www.law.cornell.edu/wex/consumer_ protection_laws#:~:text=The%20Federal%20government%20 oversees%20antitrust,Federal%20law%20in%20many%20areas.

258. "Worker representation on corporate boards of directors," Wikipedia, accessed October 30, 2023, https://en.wikipedia.org/wiki/Worker_ representation_on_corporate_boards_of_directors#:~:text=In%20 2018%2C%20a%20majority%20of,is%20often%20called%20 %22codetermination%22.

259. "What is an ESOP?" Transactional Law Clinic Collaborative, accessed October 30, 2023, https://www.wcl.american.edu/academics/ experientialedu/clinical/theclinics/elc/tlcc/for-businesses-nonprofits/ esops-info-sheet/#:~:text=•,flexibly%20out%20of%20the%20business.

260. "Cooperative identity, values and principles," International Cooperative Alliance, accessed October 30, 2023, https://ica.coop/en/cooperatives/ cooperative-identity

261. Nadeau, E.G., *Strengthening the Cooperative Community*, The Cooperative Society Project, 2021, https://thecooperativesociety.org/book-strengthening-the-cooperative-community/

262. "Wall Street and the Stock Exchanges: Historical Resources," Library of Congress Resource Guides, accessed March 24, 2024, https://guides.loc.gov/wall-street-history/exchanges#:~:text=In%20the%20beginning%20there%20were,the%20Bank%20of%20New%20York.

263. Dave Grace and Associates, op. cit. (Endnote 180)

264. Ibid.

265. "Global Mutual Market Share 10," https://www.icmif.org/global-mutual-market-share-10/#:~:text=The%20report%20also%20highlights%20that,a%2013%25%20growth%20since%202012.

266. Dave Grace and Associates, op. cit. (Endnote 180)

267. Wan, Andrew, "16 Microfinance Statistics You Need to Know for 2024," Fit Small Business, January 8, 2024, https://fitsmallbusiness.com/microfinance-statistics/#:~:text=There%20Are%20More%20Than%2010%2C000,microfinance%20institutions%20throughout%20the%20world.

268. Srinivas, Hari, "Microfinance - Credit Lending Models," Continuing Research Series E-059. The Global Development Research Center, June 2015. https://www.gdrc.org/icm/model/model-fulldoc.html

269. "Industrial Agriculture and Small-scale Farming," Global Agriculture.org, accessed March 31, 2024, https://www.globalagriculture.org/report-topics/industrial-agriculture-and-small-scale-farming.html

270. "For Up to 800 Million Rural Poor, a Strong World Bank Commitment to Agriculture," World Bank, November 12, 2014 https://www.worldbank.org/en/news/feature/2014/11/12/for-up-to-800-million-rural-poor-a-strong-world-bank-commitment-to-agriculture#:~:text=About%2078%20percent%20of%20the%20world%27s%20poor%20people—%20close%20to,plates%20and%20make%20a%20living.

271.   Dave Grace and Associates, op. cit. (Endnote 180)

272.   "Food buying groups," Sustain, accessed April 20,2024, https://www.
       sustainweb.org/foodcoopstoolkit/buyingclubs/

273.   "Celebrating the 80th Anniversary of the Rural Electrification
       Administration," Posted by Brandon McBride, Administrator,
       USDA Rural Utilities Service in Rural USDA Results,
       May 20, 2016, https://www.usda.gov/media/blog/2016/05/20/
       celebrating-80th-anniversary-rural-electrification-administration

274.   Cozzie, Laura et al, "For the first time in decades, the number of people
       without access to electricity is set to increase in 2022," International
       Energy Agency, November 3, 2022, https://www.iea.org/commentaries/
       for-the-first-time-in-decades-the-number-of-people-without-access-to-
       electricity-is-set-to-increase-in-2022

275.   Dave Grace and Associates, op. cit. (Endnote 180)

276.   "Condos and co-ops: Uniforms of housing," US Department of Housing
       and Urban Development, Summer 2003, https://www.huduser.gov/
       periodicals/ushmc/summer03/summary_2.html#:~:text=Half%20of%20
       the%205%20million,more%20condos%20and%20co%2Dops.

277.   "About HOA-USA," Hoa-usa.com, accessed March 31, 2024, https://
       hoa-usa.com/about/

278.   Ibid.

279.   "Social cooperative," Wikipedia, accessed March 31, 2024, https://
       en.wikipedia.org/wiki/Social_cooperative#:~:text=An%20Italian%20
       social%20cooperative%20is,a%20social%20service%20as%20members.

280.   "Social economy in the EU," European commission, accessed
       March 31, 2024, https://single-market-economy.ec.europa.eu/sectors/
       proximity-and-social-economy/social-economy-eu_en#:~:text=There%20
       are%202.8%20million%20social,work%20for%20social%20economy%20
       enterprises

281. Scholz, Trebor, "Exploring Italian Social Cooperatives with Vera Negri Zamagni: Lessons for Platform Cooperatives," Platform Cooperativism Consortium, March 27, 2023, https://platform.coop/blog/exploring-italian-social-cooperatives-lessons-for-platform-cooperatives/

282. "The 17 goals," United Nations, accessed March 31, 2024, https://sdgs.un.org/goals

283. "Conservation Agriculture," Food and Agriculture Organization of the United Nations, accessed March 31, 2024, https://www.fao.org/conservation-agriculture/overview/what-is-conservation-agriculture/en/

284. "2023 Global Health Care Outlook," Deloitte, retrieved October 30, 2023, https://www.deloitte.com/global/en/Industries/life-sciences-health-care/analysis/global-health-care-outlook.html

285. Nadeau, E.G., "The First Mile: The Potential for Community-Based Health Cooperatives in Developing Countries," The Cooperative Society Project, accessed March 31, 2024, https://thecooperativesociety.org/wp-content/uploads/2020/02/12212-the-first-mile-community-based-health-cooperatives-.pdf

286. Cozzie, Laura et al, op. cit., (Endnote 274)

287. Nadeau, E.G., "Community Solar Cooperatives in Developing Countries," The Cooperative Society Project, May 2019, https://thecooperativesociety.org/wp-content/uploads/2020/09/190328-Community-solar-cooperatives.pdf

288. Nadeau, E.G. and Luc Nadeau, "The Role of Forestry Cooperatives in Climate Change Mitigation," The Cooperative Society Project, March 2016, https://thecooperativesociety.org/wp-content/uploads/2020/02/237e5-the-role-of-forestry-cooperatives-in-climate-change-mitigation.pdf

289. "The global cooperative network," International Cooperative Alliance, accessed March 31, 2024, https://www.ica.coop/en/about-us/our-members/global-cooperative-network

290. "Federation of Southern Cooperatives/Land Assistance Fund," accessed March 31, 2024, https://www.federation.coop

291. "CooperationWorks!: The Cooperative Development Network," Cooperation Works!, accessed March 31, 2024, https://cooperationworks.coop

292. "Mondragon, 2018 Annual Report," Mondragon Corporation, accessed March 31, 2024, https://www.mondragon-corporation.com/wp-content/themes/mondragon/docs/eng/annual-report-2018.pdf

293. Nadeau, op. cit. (Endnote 261)

294. Hadfield, Miles, "New trouble for Mondragon as two industrial co-ops leave the fold," February 1, 2023, https://www.thenews.coop/167739/sector/worker-coops/new-trouble-for-mondragon-as-two-industrial-co-ops-leave-the-fold/

295. Nadeau, op. cit. (Endnote 261)

296. "What cooperatives can do!," US Overseas Cooperative Development Council, accessed April 1, 2024, https://ocdc.coop

297. "Welcome to cooperatives in development," Cooperatives Europe, accessed April 1, 2024, https://coopseurope.coop/development/index.html

298. "Survival of the richest: How we must tax the super-rich now to fight inequality," Oxfam briefing paper, January 2023, https://oxfamilibrary.openrepository.com/bitstream/handle/10546/621477/bp-survival-of-the-richest-160123-en.pdf

299. "World Bank Group: Working for a world free of poverty," World Bank, accessed April 1, 2024, https://web.archive.org/web/20110820085425/http://siteresources.worldbank.org/EXTABOUTUS/Resources/wbgroupbrochure-en.pdf

300. "Poverty," The World Bank, accessed April 1, 2024, https://www.worldbank.org/en/topic/poverty

301. *Report of the World Commission on Environment and Development: Our Common Future,* United Nations General Assembly, 1987, https://sustainabledevelopment.un.org/content/documents/5987our-common-future.pdf

302. Beatles, "Can't Buy Me Love" lyrics, 1964, https://tinyurl.com/yrkfec2b

303. Suliman, Adela, "Can money buy happiness? Scientists say it can." *Washington Post,* March 8, 2023, https://www.washingtonpost.com/business/2023/03/08/money-wealth-happiness-study/#

304. McMillan, D. W. and D.M. Chavis, "Sense of community: A definition and theory," *Journal of Community Psychology, 14*(1), 6–23, 1986, https://psycnet.apa.org/record/1987-03834-001

305. "Social animals," Animalia, accessed April 1, 2024, https://animalia.bio/social-animals#:~:text=Social%20animals%20are%20those%20animals,groups%20and%20form%20cooperative%20societies

306. For example: Chavis, David M., "Sense of Community Index (SCI)," accessed April 1, 2024, https://scales.arabpsychology.com/s/sense-of-community-index-sci/#:~:text=Measures%20an%20individual%27s%20psychological%20sense,needs,%20and%20shared%20emotional%20connection.&text=This%20instrument%20can%20be%20found,document%20on%20pages%20191%2D193.

307. Ibid.

308. Nadeau, op. cit., (Endnote 285)

309. *The Millennium Development Goals Report 2015,* United Nations Development Programme, April 17, 2017, https://www.undp.org/publications/millennium-development-goals-report-2015#:~:text=The%20MDG%20Report%202015%20found,while%20acknowledging%20shortfalls%20that%20remain

310. "The SDGs in Action," United Nations Development Programme, accessed April 1, 2024, https://www.undp.org/sustainable-development-goals

311. Cummings, Mike, "Yale-led study/ Wild chimpanzees have surprisingly long life spans," *YaleNews,* March 20, 2017, https://news.yale.edu/2017/03/20/yale-led-study-wild-chimpanzees-have-surprisingly-long-life-spans

312. Choi, Charles Q., "Fossil Reveals What Last Common Ancestor of Humans and Apes Looked Like," *Scientific American,* August 10, 2017, https://www.scientificamerican.com/article/fossil-reveals-what-last-common-ancestor-of-humans-and-apes-looked-liked/

313. Harari, Yuval Noah, *Sapiens: A Brief History of Humankind,* Random House, 2011.

314. "What are the major changes that occurred during the agricultural revolution?" typeset.io, accessed April 1, 2024, https://typeset.io/questions/what-are-the-major-changes-that-occurred-during-the-1r3go2m0lt#

315. Harari, op. cit., p. 79 (Endnote 313)

316. "Peace, dignity and equality on a healthy planet," United Nations Charter (full text), Adopted June 26, 1945, https://www.un.org/en/about-us/un-charter/full-text

317. Millennium Development Goals "MDGs," World Health Organization, February 19, 2018, https://www.who.int/news-room/fact-sheets/detail/millennium-development-goals-(mdgs)

318. *The Millennium Development Goals Report 2015,* op. cit. (Endnote 309) https://www.un.org/millenniumgoals/2015_MDG_Report/pdf/MDG%20 2015%20rev%20(July%201).pdf

319. *The Sustainable Development Goals Report 2023,* op.cit. (Endnote 145)

320. Ibid.

321. Plackett, op. cit., (Endnote 49)

322. "World Population Prospects 2022: Summary of Results," United Nations Department of Economic and Social Affairs, 2022, https://www.un.org/development/desa/pd/sites/www.un.org.development.desa.pd/files/wpp2022_summary_of_results.pdf

323. Vollset, op. cit. (Endnote 247)

324. Bongaarts, John, "Human population growth and the demographic transition," Philosophical Transactions of The Royal Society, Biological Sciences, October 27, 2009, https://royalsocietypublishing.org/doi/10.1098/rstb.2009.0137

325. Bongaarts, John, "Human population growth and the demographic transition," Philosophical Transactions of the Royal Society B: Biological Sciences, October 27, 2009, https://www.ncbi.nlm.nih.gov/pmc/articles/PMC2781829/

326. Vollset, op. cit. (Endnote 247)

327. "Taxing Multinationals or Taxing Wealthy Individuals?," *World Inequality Report 2022*, December 2021, https://wir2022.wid.world/chapter-8/

328. Fontinelle, Amy, "A Brief History of Taxes in the U.S.," Investopedia.com, updated August 27, 2023, https://www.investopedia.com/articles/tax/10/history-taxes.asp#:~:text=Income%20Tax%20Rates%2C%20Then%20and%20Now&text=That%20changed%20over%20time.,as%20the%20chart%20below%20demonstrates.)

329. "Do the rich pay their fair share?" Oxfam, January 14, 2024, https://www.oxfamamerica.org/explore/stories/do-the-rich-pay-their-fair-share/

330. Picketty, Thomas, *A Brief History of Equality*, Belknap Press, 2022, https://www.hup.harvard.edu/file/feeds/PDF/9780674295469_sample.pdf

331. For example: "Ultra-millionaire tax," Warren for Senate, accessed April 1, 2024, https://elizabethwarren.com/plans/ultra-millionaire-tax#:~:text=Note%3A%20Elizabeth%20originally%20proposed%20a,on%20wealth%20above%20%241%20billion

332.	"Estate and inheritance taxes," Urban Institute, accessed April 1, 2024, https://www.urban.org/policy-centers/cross-center-initiatives/state-and-local-finance-initiative/state-and-local-backgrounders/estate-and-inheritance-taxes#:~:text=Estate%20and%20inheritance%20taxes%20are,the%20heirs%20of%20the%20deceased

333.	"OECD offers final guidance for global minimum corporate tax," Reuters, February 2, 2023, https://www.reuters.com/markets/oecd-offers-final-guidance-global-minimum-corporate-tax-2023-02-02/#:~:text=In%20the%20deepest%20overhaul%20of,countries%20that%20have%20lower%20rates

334.	Bunn, Daniel and Sean Bray, "The Latest on the Global Tax Agreement," Tax Foundation, December 15, 2023, https://taxfoundation.org/global-tax-agreement/#:~:text=On%20July%201st%2C%202021%2C%20over,tax%20competition%20has%20been%20done

335.	Zucman, Gabriel, "It's Time to Tax the Billionaires," *New York Times*, May 3, 2024, https://www.nytimes.com/interactive/2024/05/03/opinion/global-billionaires-tax.html#

336.	"United States sanctions," Wikipedia, accessed April 1, 2024, https://en.wikipedia.org/wiki/United_States_sanctions

337.	"Negative income tax," Wikipedia, accessed April 1, 2024, https://en.wikipedia.org/wiki/Negative_income_tax#:~:text=The%20negative%20income%20tax%20was,the%20Mincome%20Experiment%20were%20positive

338.	"Redistribution of income and wealth," Wikipedia, accessed April 1, 2024, https://en.wikipedia.org/wiki/Redistribution_of_income_and_wealth#:~:text=Redistribution%20of%20income%20and%20wealth%20is%20the%20transfer%20of%20income,confiscation%2C%20divorce%20or%20tort%20law

339. Huseynli, Aytakin and Michael Sherraden, "Child Well-Being Policies in Post-Soviet Countries: The Potential of Child Development Accounts," Center for Social Development, Brown School at Washington University in St. Louis, June 13, 2023, https://openscholarship.wustl.edu/cgi/viewcontent.cgi?article=1946&context=csd_research

340. "Asset Building – Frequently Asked Questions," Center for Social Development, Washington University in St. Louis, https://csd.wustl.edu/asset-building-faq/

341. Huseynli, Aytakin and Michael Sherraden, op. cit. (Endnote 339)

342. Ibid.

343. *The Sustainable Development Goals Report 2023,* op. cit. (Endnote 145)

344. Ibid.

345. "Climate Action," United Nations, accessed April 29,2024, https://www.un.org/sustainabledevelopment/climate-action/#:~:text=Goal%2013%20calls%20for%20urgent,well%20below%202%20degrees%20Celsius

346. "Hottest July ever signals 'era of global boiling has arrived' says UN chief," July 27, 2023, *UN News,* https://news.un.org/en/story/2023/07/1139162

347. "2023 was the world's warmest year on record, by far," *NOAA News,* January 12, 2024, https://www.noaa.gov/news/2023-was-worlds-warmest-year-on-record-by-far#:~:text=It%27s%20official%3A%202023%20was%20the,a%20record%20low%20in%202023

348. "Analysis: Is it actually hotter now than any time in the last 100,000 years?" PBS NewsHour, July 29, 2023, https://www.pbs.org/newshour/science/analysis-is-it-actually-hotter-now-than-any-time-in-the-last-100000-years

349. D'Andrea, Aaron, "Wildfires burned 18.5M hectares of land in 2023. What will happen come thaw?" *Global News,* updated December 30, 2023, https://globalnews.ca/news/10141857/canada-wildfires-side-effects/

350. "Tracking Canada's Extreme 2023 Fire Season," Earth Observatory, NASA, June 1-July 23, 2023, https://earthobservatory.nasa.gov/images/151985/tracking-canadas-extreme-2023-fire-season

351. Faiola, Anthony and Elinda Labropoulou, "How wildfires are threatening the Mediterranean way of life," *Washington Post,* updated September 4, 2023, https://www.washingtonpost.com/world/2023/09/02/greece-fires-2023-rhodes/

352. "Death toll from flash floods in Indian Himalayas climbs to 74 with at least 100 still missing," CNN, October 9, 2023, https://www.cnn.com/2023/10/09/asia/india-flood-sikkim-glacier-climate-intl/index.html

353. Noor, Dhama and Oliver Milman, "Fury after Exxon chief says public to blame for climate failures," *The Guardian,* March 4, 2024, https://www.theguardian.com/us-news/2024/mar/04/exxon-chief-public-climate-failures

354. Critchlow, Andrew, "CERAWEEK: Saudi Aramco CEO says oil phaseout is a 'fantasy' in transition rebuttal," S&P Global Commodity Insights, March 18, 2024, https://www.spglobal.com/commodityinsights/en/market-insights/latest-news/oil/031824-ceraweek-saudi-aramco-ceo-says-oil-phase-out-a-fantasy-in-transition-rebuttal#:~:text=Saudi%20Aramco%20CEO%20Amin%20Hassan,by%20S%26P%20Global%20in%20Houston

355. *The Carbon Majors Database Launch Report,* InfluenceMap, April 2024, p. 31, https://influencemap.org/site//data/000/027/Carbon_Majors_Launch_Report.pdf

356. Butts, Dylan, "China accounted for two-thirds of new global coal plant capacity in 2023, report finds," CNBC, April 14, 2024, https://www.cnbc.com/2024/04/15/china-boosts-global-coal-power.html

357. Patterson, Nicholas, "What is Environmental Sustainability? Goals with Examples," Southern New Hampshire University, January 16, 2024, https://www.snhu.edu/about-us/newsroom/stem/what-is-environmental-sustainability

358. "Human ecology," Wikipedia, op. cit. (Endnote 15)

359. "Is it too late to prevent climate change?" NASA Facts, accessed January 28, 2024, https://climate.nasa.gov/faq/16/is-it-too-late-to-prevent-climate-change/

360. Pester, Patrick, "When did scientists first warn humanity about climate change?" *Live Science,* December 12, 2021, https://www.livescience.com/humans-first-warned-about-climate-change

361. "United Nations Conference on Environment and Development, Rio de Janeiro, Brazil, 3-14 June 1992," United Nations, accessed April 2, 2024, https://www.un.org/en/conferences/environment/rio1992

362. "United Nations Framework Convention on Climate Change," Wikipedia, accessed April 2, 2024, https://en.wikipedia.org/wiki/United_Nations_Framework_Convention_on_Climate_Change

363. Ibid.

364. "What is the Paris Agreement?" United Nations Framework Convention on Climate Change, accessed April 2, 2024, https://unfccc.int/process-and-meetings/the-paris-agreement/the-paris-agreement

365. "Key aspects of the Paris Agreement," United Nations Framework Convention on Climate Change, accessed April 2, 2024, https://unfccc.int/most-requested/key-aspects-of-the-paris-agreement#:~:text=The%20Paris%20Agreement%27s%20central%20aim,further%20to%201.5%20degrees%20Celsius.

366. Harvey, Fiona and Ajit Niranjan, "What is the UAE COP28 plan of climate action?" *The Guardian,* July 13, 2023, https://www.theguardian.com/environment/2023/jul/13/what-is-the-uae-cop28-plan-of-climate-action#:~:text=At%20Cop28%2C%20governments%20will%20conduct,NDCs%20–%20they%20made%20in%20Paris.

367. "1.5 degree climate pledge 'on life support', Guterres tells leaders during frank exchanges," *UN News,* September 21, 2022, https://news.un.org/en/story/2022/09/1127381

368. "The CAT Thermometer," Climate Action Tracker, updated December 5, 2023, https://climateactiontracker.org/global/cat-thermometer/

369. Xue, Yujie, "Climate change: global warming of 2.7 degrees will expose 2 billion people to 'dangerous heat' by end of century, study shows," May 22, 2023, *South China Morning Post,* https://www.scmp.com/business/article/3221423/climate-change-global-warming-27-degrees-will-expose-2-billion-people-dangerous-heat-end-century#

370. "Deloitte research reveals inaction on climate change could cost the world's economy US$178 trillion by 2070," Deloitte, May 23, 2022, https://www.deloitte.com/global/en/about/press-room/deloitte-research-reveals-inaction-on-climate-change-could-cost-the-world-economy-us-dollar-178-trillion-by-2070.html

371. "The costs of delay," Energy Innovation, January 2021, https://energyinnovation.org/wp-content/uploads/2021/01/Cost_of_Delay.pdf

372. Rajagopalan, Rishikesh and Tucker Reals "COP28 climate conference president Sultan al-Jaber draws more fire over comments on fossil fuels," CBS News, updated December 4, 2023, https://www.cbsnews.com/news/cop28-climate-conference-president-sultan-al-jaber-fossil-fuels/#:~:text=Dr.,National%20Oil%20Company%20(ADNOC).

373. Calverley, Dan and Kevin Anderson, *Phaseout Pathways for Fossil Fuel Production within Paris-compliant carbon budget: Research Report,* The University of Manchester Research, March 11, 2022, https://pure.manchester.ac.uk/ws/portalfiles/portal/213256008/Tyndall_Production_Phaseout_Report_final_text_3_.pdf

374. "The CAT Thermometer," op. cit. (Endnote 368)

375. Herring, David and Rebecca Lindsey, "Can we slow or even reverse global warming?" Climate.gov, October 12, 2022, https://www.climate.gov/news-features/climate-qa/can-we-slow-or-even-reverse-global-warming

376. "COP28 Agreement Signals 'Beginning of the End' of the Fossil Fuel Era," *UN Climate Change News,* December 13, 2023, https://unfccc.int/news/cop28-agreement-signals-beginning-of-the-end-of-the-fossil-fuel-era

377. "First global stocktake," United Nations Framework Convention on Climate Change, December 13, 2023, https://unfccc.int/sites/default/files/resource/cma2023_L17_adv.pdf

378. "Fit for 55: Delivering on the proposals," European Commission, accessed April 2, 2024, https://commission.europa.eu/strategy-and-policy/priorities-2019-2024/european-green-deal/delivering-european-green-deal/fit-55-delivering-proposals_en

379. "EU Climate Action Tracker," Climate Action Tracker, accessed February 6, 2024, https://climateactiontracker.org/countries/eu/

380. Ibid.

381. "US state carbon pricing policies," Center for Climate and Energy Solutions, accessed April 2, 2024, https://www.c2es.org/document/us-state-carbon-pricing-policies/

382. "UNCTAD calls for urgent support to developing countries to attract massive investment in clean energy," Unctad, July 5, 2023, https://unctad.org/press-material/unctad-calls-urgent-support-developing-countries-attract-massive-investment-clean

383. Taylor, Matthew, "Taxing big fossil fuel firms 'could raise \$900bn in climate finance by 2030,'" The Guardian, April 28, 2024, https://www.theguardian.com/environment/2024/apr/29/taxing-big-fossil-fuel-firms-raise-billions-climate-finance

384. Miriri, Duncan, "African leaders seek record World Bank financing to combat climate change," Reuters, April 29, 2024, https://www.reuters.com/world/africa/african-leaders-seek-record-world-bank-financing-combat-climate-change-2024-04-29/

385. "COP28 concludes with historic agreement to try to tackle the climate crisis," Reliefweb, December 13, 2023, https://reliefweb.int/report/world/cop28-concludes-historic-agreement-try-tackle-climate-crisis#:~:text=Warnings%20for%20All-,The%20United%20Nations%20Climate%20Change%20conference%2C%20COP28%2C%20has%20concluded%20with,finance%20for%20the%20most%20vulnerable.

386. *IPCC Sixth Assessment Report, Working Group 1: The Physical Science Basis, Summary for Policymakers,* International Plant Protection Convention, accessed April 2, 2024, https://www.ipcc.ch/report/ar6/wg1/chapter/summary-for-policymakers/

387. Hirji, Zahra, "The World Is on Track to Warm 3 Degrees Celsius This Century. Here's What That Means." BuzzFeed News, October 30, 2021, https://www.buzzfeednews.com/article/zahrahirji/global-warming-3-degrees-celsius-impact

388. Rentschler, Jun et al., "Flood risk already affects 1.81 billion people. Climate change and unplanned urbanization could worsen exposure," World Bank Blogs, June 28, 2022, https://blogs.worldbank.org/climatechange/flood-risk-already-affects-181-billion-people-climate-change-and-unplanned

389. Hirji, op. cit. (Endnote 387)

390. Ibid.

391. Rentschler, Jun et al, op. cit. (Endnote 388)

392. "Ten years of clean energy start-ups," International Energy Agency, July 23, 2021, https://www.iea.org/articles/ten-years-of-clean-energy-start-ups

393. Hernick, Charles and Lisa Jacobson, "The Decade That Made Clean Energy," Morning Consult, February 18, 2020, https://morningconsult.com/opinions/decade-that-made-clean-energy/

394. Richie, Hannah and Pablo Rosado, "Fossil fuels," Our World in Data, revised January 2024, https://ourworldindata.org/fossil-fuels#global-fossil-fuel-consumption

395. "Swedish Immigration to the U.S.," Minnesota Historical Society, accessed April 2, 2024, https://www.mnhs.org/newspapers/swedishamerican-migration#:~:text=During%20the%201880s%20alone%2C%20some,persons%20in%20the%20United%20States

396. "Politics of Norway," Wikipedia, accessed April 2, 2024, https://en.wikipedia.org/wiki/Politics_of_Norway#:~:text=The%20Norwegian%20constitution%2C%20signed%20by,96%2C%2097%2C%2099)

397. *Democracy Index 2023*, op. cit. (Endnote 150)

398. "Indicators of economy in Sweden," World data.info, accessed April 2, 2024, https://www.worlddata.info/europe/sweden/economy.php#:~:text=Worldwide%20gross%20domestic%20product%20in,23%20of%20the%20major%20economies.

399. "Svensk Kooperation – Tillsammans för kooperativt företagande," Svensk Kooperation, accessed April 2, 2024, https://svenskkooperation.se/about-swedish-cooperation/?lang=english

400. "Sweden, Social Values," Sustainable Governance Indicators, accessed April 2, 2024, https://www.sgi-network.org/2022/Sweden/Social_Policies

401. *Democracy Index 2023*, op. cit. (Endnote 150)

402. Ibid.

403. "Arab petrostates must prepare their citizens for a post-oil future. Better schools and a political voice would be a start." *The Economist*, February 9, 2023, https://www.economist.com/leaders/2023/02/09/arab-petrostates-must-prepare-their-citizens-for-a-post-oil-future

404. *Democracy Index 2023*, op. cit. (Endnote 150)

405. Nadeau, op. cit. (Endnote 261)

406. "UN resolution calls for a second International Year of Cooperatives in 2025," International Cooperative and Mutual Insurance Federation, November 20, 2023, https://tinyurl.com/4dfvb9bb

407. "Advancing social justice, promoting decent work," International Labour Organization, accessed April 3, 2024, https://www.ilo.org/global/lang--en/index.htm

408. "COP28 Agreement Signals 'Beginning of the End' of the Fossil Fuel Era," op. cit. (Endnote 376)

409. "Cooperative identity, values & principles," International Cooperative Alliance, accessed April 25, 2024, https://ica.coop/en/cooperatives/cooperative-identity#:~:text=Cooperatives%20are%20based%20on%20the,responsibility%20and%20caring%20for%20others

410. Ibid.

Index

D